Also from Rivkah Lambert Adler, Ph.D,

Lighting Up The Nations:
Jewish Responsibility Towards the Nations
Today and in the Messianic Era

Ten From The Nations:
Torah Awakening Among Non-Jews

100 Days of Thanking Hashem:
A Jewish Gratitude Journal

ADRIFT AMONG THE NATIONS

Between Christianity and Torah

Edited by

Rivkah Lambert Adler, Ph.D,

Adrift Among The Nations: Between Christianity and Torah

Copyright © 2025 by Rivkah Lambert Adler, Ph.D.

For permission requests, write to rivkah@kotevet.com.

ISBN: 978-0-9993789-8-4

Advanced Praise for
Adrift Among the Nations

A must-read for anyone who has ever asked the question, "Is it possible to have a relationship with G-d outside of Jesus?" These are honest questions which deserve honest answers. The clarity of those of us who have left the Church community and are asking the unanswered questions will find this book essential in our request for the truth of our own spiritual journeys. There is so much that we were not prepared to deal with in our journey to a higher form of spirituality that we have found outside of Christianity and organized religion, that we have often felt alienated and disappointed because of our choice to follow the path of Torah.

This book and the issues it addresses will help us understand a broader perspective and alternatives to yet another organized religious experience.

The biggest hurdle in leaving a safe community such as Christianity is to feel comfortable with our decision to leave Christianity without feeling alienated by G-d. Yet, the alienation is real, whether from family, community, or our previous way of thinking. The journey always begins with honesty.

This book is essential for those who are not only believing in a creed, but living their creed. We must begin with what we know, and then move forward, honestly seeking truth, no matter where it may be found. – **Jim Busch**, moderator of Following G-d, Out of Christianity (A return to Torah Teaching) Facebook group

This book is a **powerful, emotionally engaging read**. I found myself reading and reliving my own experiences in the words of these souls, as they recounted the details of their experiences in leaving their former faith communities. There are people out there who are silently considering the cost of leaving their faith community. This book will be a treasure to them, confirming that others have done the same, and they can try to understand and prepare for the next steps. May God continue to guide us all closer to Him. – **Ben Edward**, moderator of Following G-d, Out of Christianity (A return to Torah Teaching) Facebook group

I have great respect, admiration, and, truthfully, awe for the authors of the autobiographical statements in this volume. It took a great deal of courage to begin their journeys away from the faith they knew and step toward the unknown. That journey begins with a very dangerous step: to start asking questions!

Learning the answers and surprisingly finding those answers in a minority and isolated people can be a great shock. It often leads to loneliness, families divided, communities lost, and immense emotional and spiritual sacrifice, but amazingly, they remain on their journeys. Some voices here are very new and raw, while others renounced their former religion a long time ago. I wish each of these authors, Chazak v'Amatz, to be strong and courageous!

Thank you, Rivkah Lambert Adler, for assembling these here. The world needs to hear these stories and the myriads like them as the world gets closer to the fulfillment of Jeremiah 16:19 and Zechariah 8:23. Your work honors the path of those brave souls who walk away from familiarity in search of something eternal. It stands as a welcome to the Jewish people and a validation of those Jews who sacrificed and suffered as God's servants.

May these stories inspire others to start their journeys, may they validate those who remain on their journeys and those who have fully found their home in Judaism with the Jewish People! – **Rabbi Stuart Federow**, author of *Judaism and Christianity: A Contrast*, and *The REAL Reasons Why Jews Don't Believe In Jesus*.

Having traveled this path myself - from the pulpit of Christian ministry to a life anchored in Torah - I recognize the courage, heartbreak, and holy yearning woven through *Adrift Among the Nations*. These stories don't preach or proselytize; they testify. **They give voice to a quiet, growing population of souls torn between loyalty to a former faith family and loyalty to Torah-based truth.** This book doesn't offer answers - it offers solidarity, and sometimes, that's exactly what's needed most. – **Gavriel Sanders**, International speaker and educator

Adrift Among the Nations is a **deeply moving and courageous** collection of stories from women who have left prior beliefs to embrace the Torah and move closer to Hashem. Dr. Rivkah Lambert Adler's **poignant anthology captures the spiritual, emotional, and communal challenges of this transformative journey.** Through raw, relatable narratives...many from Adler's own Torah study group...it offers solace and solidarity to truth-seekers navigating faith and identity. A palatable beacon of hope and connection to the Jewish people. A must-read for anyone drawn to the call of Torah. – **Victor Schultz**, founder (MishnahWalk.com)

To make known Your way on earth, among all nations Your salvation. (Psalms 67:3)

If we stop for a moment and think about the past 80 years of history, we are living through unprecedented times. After the world wrote us off as finished, the revival of Jewish sovereignty in our ancestral homeland after nearly 2000 years was clearly providential. The countless miracles that allowed us to overcome dire challenges and build a thriving nation have been no less breathtaking.

We experienced another worldwide upheaval beginning in the 1960s. Many thousands of Jewish people who grew up disconnected from their spiritual heritage began returning passionately to the faith of their ancestors. This movement continues to this day, and the returnees have left an indelible impact upon the broader Jewish society.

And then, beginning about a generation ago, we began witnessing perhaps the most unexpected development. **Growing numbers of people deeply involved in the Church are being drawn to the light of Torah.** Some are embracing Judaism as their spiritual path; others are drawn to the burgeoning Noahide movement. Many simply come to see themselves as Gentiles who desire to come close to the Creator by living according to the teachings of the Tanach.

I know this movement is real because I've been in contact with hundreds of these individuals. I am inspired by their sincerity and devotion and humbled by the incredible sacrifices they make in pursuit of truth.

Over the past decade, Rivkah Lambert Adler has had her finger on the pulse of this phenomenon. Her latest book, exploring this spiritual upheaval, *Adrift Among the Nations: Between Christianity and Torah,* chronicles the poignant stories of those who have gone through the gut-wrenching experience of re-evaluating their faith in light of the Torah and finding it wanting.

This is **an important and inspiring book** because it shines a spotlight on part of the process of geulah (redemption) that many are unaware of. My prayer is that it will lead many Jewish people to embrace more intimately our Biblical role of being a light to the nations and I thank Dr. Adler for being a tireless advocate for universal Torah awareness. – **Rabbi Michael Skobac**, Director of Education and Counseling, Jews for Judaism, Canada

When I wrote *Leaving Jesus*, I had no idea how my family and friends would react. I always hoped they would want to examine Christianity to determine its validity as I did. I didn't expect them to react adversely. I wasn't prepared for the reactions I received and I had no resources to turn to help me deal with the emotions I would feel myself. I wish I had *Adrift Among The Nations* when I was leaving Jesus. This is the companion to my book *Leaving Jesus* you definitely need. – **James Wood, Jr.,** author of *Leaving Jesus: A Book Every Christian Should Have Read Before They Believed in Jesus*

Praise for Lighting Up The Nations

Rachel is weeping for her children, but Redemption is coming! We can sense it. As a non-Jew, I am grateful for people like Dr. Rivkah Lambert Adler who are bringing awareness and building bridges between the Jewish people and those thirsty ones who wish to drink from Judah's well of knowledge regarding Torah. While this book was primarily written for a Jewish audience, mature, Torah-aware (non-Jewish) believers in Hashem will gain a deeper understanding of the Jewish heart and mind as they read Lighting Up The Nations. Understandably, it will take a great deal of patient willingness to build trust and understanding between Jews and the nations, but those brave Jewish souls who are willing to step out are prophetically fulfilling their role as a Light to the Nations. These are exciting times, and I want to personally thank those Jewish lights who recognize the souls within those of us who deeply desire the restoration of all of Israel. – **Chasity Galyon**

The Torah tells us that we are here not only to elevate our souls, but to transform the physical world into a Divine garden where God's essence is fully revealed. At that time, the sages say, all of humanity will seek to learn Torah and all will serve God as one.

Throughout the centuries of exile, the Jewish people risked their lives to keep the Torah. It was impossible to imagine that millions of non-Jews would someday start seeking the Torah's wisdom with a passionate hunger and thirst. And yet, that day has arrived. Sincere, humble souls from among the nations are seeking a deeper truth and a new relationship with God that only the Torah can provide. According to many of the greatest rabbis of our generation, including the Lubavitcher Rebbe, a fundamental part of the Jewish mission in these times of redemption is to teach the peoples of the world Torah-true wisdom, helping them to take their place in creating an inhabitable world which ultimately will be filled with the knowledge of God like water covers the ocean bed (Habakkuk 2:14).

Such a foundational change does not come easily to most of us. We, as Jews, need to more deeply understand and internalize our new role. Lighting Up

The Nations is an important step in helping us do exactly that. – **Shifra Chana Hendrie**, Founder and CEO of The Gate of Unity (gateofunity.com)

An absolutely wonderful book to gain understanding into an unprecedented paradigm shift taking place in the Orthodox Jewish community in their approach to geulah responsive to the multitudes of non-Jewish Torah seekers who are awakening out of the Nations. It is written very much like a legal brief that is submitted to a court, which is written in a very clear concise, and direct manner, but enveloped in a warm passionate vulnerable plea to fellow Orthodox Jews to join them in pursuit of their divine mandate and prophetic responsibilities to those of the 10 tribes, as well as, those from the Nations seeking to embrace a Torah specific life. It is refreshing to know that the paradigm is changing for both Jews and non-Jews. You will cry, rejoice and nod your head in agreement at the astounding statements presented. I want to read it again and again because I want to ingest all the thoughts contained within. You will appreciate all the link references to have direct contact with the writers who are completely open to being an advocate and teacher for all those seeking the Father's heart. I believe this book will be a catalyst to a profound prophetic awakening and paradigm shift for the geulah of Jews and non-Jews alike. – **Keleigh J. Mollak**

Dr. Adler puts together an excellent resource that should challenge all streams of Judaism, but especially normative Orthodoxy. Orthodox Judaism has majestically and courageously maintained itself, the Jewish tradition and our Torah sources of wisdom - against historical, political, social, economic and military forces for 2,000 years. Social and political opportunities now face us in the modern era, in which we need to "come out of the closet" of insularity, so that we can fulfill our mission as a light onto the nations. Mere survival (and even our thriving) is no deep teacher in terms of the Jewish mission statement from Hashem.

The rabbis and educators who courageously go against that insularity we developed to survive, are waking up to the fact that we are a living miracle. That miracle needs to be acknowledged with acting on and with our Torah. The Jewish people and our tradition has survived all comers, for longer than science and history can neatly explain. That seems to indicate the strength of our tradition, faith, and Torah. Our tradition teaches the goals of Geulah - Redemption. Before we can physically leave the exile and make aliyah, we need to make an aliyah of the mind and spirit: a time to actually assume the role of teachers to mankind, where there are voluntary, non-conversionary agendas and good will. We need to do it from an internal Jewish spirit, not some foreign, external influence.

Some estimate there are as many as 60 million people worldwide that have honest questions as to how the Torah / Tanach relate to them, how our texts answer the many questions that exist in the non-Jewish world of faith. Many non-Jews who have dabbled in Jewish Torah sources are amazed that we can actually answer questions they were taught are unnecessary, unwanted and unexplainable. They are naively surprised that we have kept it "secret". This is our wisdom among the nations. Hashem saved us from our enemies, has allowed the resurrection of the 3rd commonwealth of Israel to flourish, the Jewish people continue to grow in Holy Land, many in the well-meaning non-Jewish world wonder about that. Hashem has given us an opportunity to unleash the wisdom we faithfully kept. Hillel said: "If I am not for myself, who will be for me? If I am only for myself, what am I? And if not now, when?" Maybe we need to open up, step out of our comfort zone, be more approachable to truth-seekers from the nations, and help foster the Redemption by proactively earning it with living up to our mission statement. We trust in the Torah and Hashem, that He did not give us a test we cannot pass. This is our time. – **Alan Hoffman**

Praise for Ten From The Nations:
Torah Awakening Among Non Jews

Couldn't put this book down! I enjoyed reading how other non-Jews came to love the Torah and how similar some of their experiences were to mine. But, more than that, I cried when I read how my Jewish brethren are beginning to notice something big is starting to happen world-wide and many are open to it. This book is uplifting, encouraging, and validating. Rivkah has done a wonderful work and is very courageous to bridge a 2000 year divide. – **B. Smith**

[T]he stories from these brave witnesses are crucial to understanding that Divine restoration is underway and that the people of God should arise and prepare for the next steps. The discerning reader will be provoked to much prayer for wisdom and discernment as to how to respond to this evidence. I salute Dr. Adler for her courage! – **Cathy Helms**

This is a wonderful book of individual stories of people from many walks of life coming to similar conclusions independently of one another. It's well written and desperately needed today... Thank you Rivkah Lambert Adler for being so brave and willing to engage in dialogue with those that love the God of Abraham, Isaac, and Jacob just as much as you do. I hope it will be used as an instrument for peace among all of Israel. I can also see that as fast as people are changing and returning to a love of Torah, Truth, a True understanding of the God of Israel, and the People of Israel this book will be a history book in no time at all. Their stories are just a drop in the bucket of countless others. It's so nice to have them written down giving legitimacy to so many people who thought they were the only ones. YOU'RE NOT!!! Must read folks!!! – **Jeremy Landauer**

Dr. Rivkah Lambert Adler has courageously dared to become the lightning rod around which an AMAZING conversation is taking place. Over the last 30 to 40 years a quiet revolution has begun within both Christendom and Judaism that is beginning to be felt very publicly and Adler's important work, Ten From the Nations, begins to chart the breadth, width and depth of this revolution. Like an iceberg, with 90% of its mass hidden under the waters, a Torah Awakening has been happening across the globe. Christians are quietly waking, as if from deep slumber, to the continued relevance of the Torah, the five books of Moses and the contained Instructions in Righteousness. Both Jews and Christians are seeing this growing, even accelerating, shift and grappling with its significance... I encourage reading and wrestling with the contents of this book! – **Pete Rambo**

This Book was Wonderful, Timely and Challenging. I read all of it in about 4-5 hours, which was amazing because I cried through several pages. I could identify with the Journey of many coming from a Christian background. The struggles and blessings many have found in Keeping the Torah. Just to have our Jewish brethren take a closer look at us and wonder why or how this came to be thrills my soul... I appreciate the tremendous Chutzpah of Dr. Rivkah Lambert Adler in compiling the individual contributions and opinions. The fact that these Two groups can find Holy Ground in the Torah is nothing less than Miraculous. The Jews have been at this for thousands of years and we have much to learn from them, having just rediscovered this treasure ourselves. – **Mary Stowell**

Contents

APPENDIX A

APPENDIX B

Dedication

This book is dedicated to the women from the Nations who study Torah with me each week. I marvel at their courage, their openness and the many ways that they honor the Torah in their lives. Their support for me as a Torah teacher enables me to fulfill my God-given role to be a light to the Nations.

"We must let go of the life we have planned, so as to accept the one that is waiting for us."

— JOSEPH CAMPBELL,
writer and professor of literature (1904-1987)

"Sometimes you have to lose yourself to find yourself."

— BRYANT MCGILL,
best-selling author and social media influencer

Acknowledgments

This is my opportunity to publicly thank:

The Creator and Sustainer of the Universe, who never stops pointing out the path upon which He wants me to walk.

Deborah Amyx, Laura Blair, Andrea Chester, Ada Davis, Ginni Gamble. Teresa Hutslar, Paushali Lass, Vanessa Ramsey and Martine Zelenak who opened up their souls so that others may have an easier time.

Shannon Nuszen who allowed me to reprint the most gut-wrenching poem from her memoir *I Once Was Lost*.

Rabbi Yishai Fleisher whose casual conversation at the pool in Beit Guvrin in July 2024 prodded me to proceed with this volume.

James Wood Jr. whose book *Leaving Jesus* was the original inspiration for *Adrift Among The Nations*.

Rabbi Ari Abramowitz who encouraged me to move ahead with this project despite my apprehensions and who talked me out of using a pseudonym.

Jim Busch, Ben Edward, Rabbi Stuart Federow, Rabbi Michael Skobac, Gavriel Sanders, Victor Schultz and James Wood Jr. who saw the value of this work and offered words of support in advance of its publication.

Editor's Introduction

But whosoever shall deny me before men, him will
I also deny before my Father which is in heaven.
(Matthew 10:33)

This book is about people raised as Christians who, despite the fearful implication of this key verse from the Book of Matthew, stopped believing in Jesus as part of their spiritual journeys.

It concerns a subset of Christians who walked away from Jesus as divine and as the messiah. It is about truth seekers who love the Creator and Sustainer of the universe and want to worship Him alone. It is about former Christians who have discovered Torah and are figuring out how it applies to them. In that sense, it's as much a Jewish book as a Christian one.

I'll be honest. It was hard for me to decide to publish this book.

From my work with current and former Christians, I knew it needed to be written, and I felt strongly that a book like this would help people who are at this delicate stage in their journeys.

But I also knew it would hurt some followers of Jesus for whom I care very much.

So I waited half a year, not wanting to alienate the Christians in my life. I briefly considered publishing under a pseudonym and asked advice from a few colleagues. Before proceeding, I even spoke to some of my Christian students, colleagues and friends about the project.

Ultimately, I decided that this was part of the story of the Torah awakening among non-Jews that needed to be told in its own volume.

Since 2014, when God brought me, an Orthodox Jewish woman living in Israel, into an awareness of the Torah awakening among non-Jews, I have been documenting the unfolding phenomenon.

In 2017, when I first published *Ten From The Nations: Torah Awakening Among Non-Jews*, many readers correctly noted that I was ***describing*** a movement rather than ***prescribing*** a path. One reviewer summed up my approach with these words: "She lets the story tell itself. She does not insert her own beliefs, prejudice, or agenda into the book."

The same is true with this book. I am neither *prescribing* a path nor proselytizing on behalf of Judaism. I'm not trying to convince Christians that their faith is wrong. Rather, I'm *describing* a stage of the journey as some people experience it. In that way, I am fulfilling my role as a journalist, documenting a phenomenon with which I am deeply engaged, even though it is not my personal story.

In my work describing the Torah awakening among non-Jews. I endeavor to open space for wrestling, rather than close space with conclusions.

This book offers support to those going through a difficult transition by sharing the stories of others who have walked this path. Exactly as I did with *Ten From The Nations*, my goal is to let these stories tell themselves.

I have a lot of compassion for people who leave the church and leave Jesus, often at significant personal cost. It's a painful step. ***Adrift Among the Nations* is about the spiritual, emotional, communal, interpersonal and psychological experience of leaving Jesus and the guilt, grieving, loss and hopefully, the rebuilding that follows.**

Most of the chapters in this modest volume were written by my own students, the women from all over the world who study Torah with me every Tuesday night on Zoom. When I first began soliciting essays, I didn't intend to have the book dominated by the stories of my own students, but that's how God directed the outcome of this project.

While acknowledging the limited demographic representation of this volume, the stories these ten women tell about their journeys are both specific to them and also meant to be relatable to others walking a similar path.

In addition to the limited demographic representation, this volume does not include chapters written by Christians who once embraced Torah and returned to their Christian roots. Those stories exist, but they are not the goal of this book.

It's also important to note that these essays represent the stories of people in different places on their journeys out of Christianity. The stories are presented in their own words and some of their ideas about Torah Judaism may not align with mainstream Jewish thought. Similarly, these stories present Christian teachings in the way the contributors understand them. Followers of Jesus, whether they attend church or not, may have a different understanding of Christian doctrine and theology.

I'd like to draw your attention to one special chapter that was *not* written by one of my students: "The Abrahamic Movement: The Ancient Jewish Faith Path You Didn't Know You're Already Almost On" by Rabbi Yishai Fleisher. In it, Fleisher proposes an entirely new religious identity for those who have left Jesus and are adrift among the nations, between Christianity and Torah.

Rivkah Lambert Adler, Ph.D.
Efrat, Israel
Iyar 5785

THE STORIES

I Just Wanted to Follow the God of Abraham, Isaac and Jacob

Deborah Amyx

I was born into a Christian family in Indiana. My uncle was the pastor of a congregation that consisted of most of my extended family, who had migrated from Kentucky to Indiana, along with other families from the hills of Kentucky. We were a congregation of about 150-200 people.

My uncle taught the whole Bible. He had visited Israel and, as a result, had a concentration on the first five books of the Hebrew Bible. He also taught Christian teachings like the trinity and we met on Sundays. We did not observe Jewish festivals. It was an independent Pentecostal church, so he could teach anything he learned, with no oversight or restrictions found in denominational churches.

My young mind at the age of four and five recognized that there is a God in heaven and I thought Jesus was like my big brother. I had no concept then of the cross. I just believed that God loved me and that He proved it by sending Jesus to die for my sins. How do I remember this? My parents divorced when I was four years old and I remember my Sunday school teachers, who only taught four- to five-year-olds. I also remember feeling abandoned and unloved without my daddy, crying in bed as I'd drift off to sleep, but remembering that God loved me and was my daddy now.

I also remember lying on the grass, trying to stare as deeply as possible into the bluest, cloudless sky so I could perhaps get a glimpse of God. I'd even talk to Him about trying to see Him. I wanted the Creator of that big, beautiful sky to be my Father. From that day forward, I depended on Him as my Father in heaven in many situations.

Because of my uncle's trips to Israel, in 1978, I decided to take modern Hebrew at the University of Maryland. I enjoyed the class, but I worked full time at a Jewish fabric store in Rockville, Maryland during my freshman year. Hearing the instructor, a native Israeli from Tel Aviv, speak my name just awed me. The sound was so beautiful! That led me to consider the idea of becoming Jewish, as I had acquired a deep love for Israel (from my uncle's teachings about the chosen people). I actually longed to be one of the chosen people.

On my long 45-minute drive to and from work, I often thought that if I didn't have to reject Jesus, I'd convert! I was already married, since age 17, to a college graduate who attended my church. It was a conservative Christian marriage. There was no way he would ever consider such a thing, so I put such thoughts aside and tried to please God by being an exceptional wife, perhaps attaining the goal of being like the Virtuous Woman of Proverbs 31.

About that time, I heard of a singer named Keith Green who was a Jewish Christian. I loved his frankness and challenge to the church to "be like Jesus." In my mind, being like Jesus was all that mattered. I understood his role to be an example of how non-Jews were to live in the world, not ever replacing the Jews, but just living in harmony with them.

I think there was a movement in the churches about that time, in the late 1970s, to get back to the "early church," which meant doing things the way Jesus's followers did things. It didn't go much farther than that for me since I became a mother. To be a mom was what I thought I was created for. I wanted to give it all my attention.

Though there were times throughout my life after the 1970s that I encountered someone Jewish or someone who taught something Jewish, I continued for decades with a mom focus. It wasn't until all my children were grown, in 2020, that I looked once again. Until that year, I truly believed that I was doing what was right, even though I had shortcomings. I understood sin as taught in the Torah. My uncle made it clear that all we had to do was repent and stop sinning. I never reconciled that with Jesus on the cross. I was comfortable with my life.

In 2020, I was in a third marriage when COVID hit the world. I immediately knew that God was calling the world to repentance. I wondered if we were in the days of Jacob's trouble, called by Christians, the "great tribulation" with an accompanying "rapture" for those who were redeemed by Jesus's blood.

I didn't know the prophets very well, though I had read through the "Old Testament" several times. I couldn't help but feel this worldwide phenomenon was happening as a call to repent. But what from? I didn't think I had intentionally sinned that I hadn't repented of already. I lived a life of repentance and stopping what I had been doing that I knew was wrong.

I began searching for prophetic teachings, which brought me to Messianic Christian teachers. One of them challenged the idea of the trinity. I was shocked and listened intently to what he had to say. He didn't say whether there was a trinity or not. But I remembered my uncle's teaching from the 1960s that the God of Abraham, Isaac and Jacob was the Creator of heaven and earth and that we must always pray only to Him.

With the idea of the trinity blown apart, I searched for more. I felt alive and couldn't get enough of learning, as the churches had meaningless homilies and nothing more. My own studies had gone by the wayside, except when I had a question, but in Christianity, questions are not welcome. It was all dry and meaningless, but these teachers were challenging me! I listened to these teachers teach Torah from the Hebrew and I learned that the Ten Commandments were different in the Hebrew scriptures. Now, I wanted to revisit what the Ten Commandments really meant in Hebrew.

In 2021, I decided to visit a synagogue, but I found a Hebrew Roots congregation that looked less intimidating on their website, so I visited there instead and was welcomed. They taught Sabbatarian ideas like Christians keeping the Sabbath and the Jewish Festivals. I didn't really know anything better, so I attended all of these in 2021, 2022 and 2023.

My marriage was a difficult one, in large part due to our different spiritual states. My husband was a Nashville musician, raised in a Methodist denomination, who didn't really take any of the scriptures seriously. When I told him that I wanted to keep Shabbat, meaning to me that I would not cook or do chores or earn money on that day, he became very upset and filed for divorce. I was devastated and frightened as I had no retirement, savings or child support to draw from to start over again. All my kids were grown. I knew God would work out things for me as I took the steps to build a new life.

In June, 2023, I listened to a man who taught about the Jewish Temple. He mentioned a public Facebook group called The Mishnah Walk that we could visit to learn more about what the Jewish sages taught. I immediately found the site and joined. It didn't seem to teach very much, but I discovered a closed community of the same Mishnah Walk community that was for members only.

We were warned that to be a member, we had to stop all avoda zara.[1] I wasn't quite sure what that was, but I guessed it had

---

[1] Hebrew for idol worship

something to do with the commandments, perhaps worshiping idols. I hesitated for a couple of days, knowing that I might have to reject Jesus. I had listened to a couple of Rabbi Tovia Singer's videos weeks before, so I finally decided that, even if it meant rejecting Jesus, I wanted to please my Father in heaven.

I knew nothing about Judaism at this point. Nothing. I just wanted to follow my God, the God of Abraham, Isaac, and Jacob, the One I had been praying to all my life, though in Christian surroundings, the One I needed and depended on to get me through all my life's struggles of abuse and divorce and learning how to be a better person. It was He who made all these things happen for my good, of that, I was sure. I was okay with the idea and when I made that promise to reject avoda zara, not knowing exactly what it meant, but determined to please Hashem, I took the plunge.

It took me all my life to get to this point. I was 64 years old by this time, with two grown sons, three grown daughters and six grandchildren.

In my situation, I had learned to mull things over and find evidence to make my decisions on my own. I did use a lot of YouTube videos in searching – listening to both sides of the debate, but I also purchased a Tanach[2] at a used bookstore. I had only websites to find information to verify what was being taught, as my limited income had to be managed carefully.

I didn't really have friends to discuss it with. I had tried to do that only once. It was in my Hebrew Roots church, after oneg[3]. We would meet around a table, about eight to ten people. We'd ask questions and discuss various topics, except mine. Every time I asked a

---

[2] Hebrew scriptures
[3] Hebrew for joy, used to refer to an informal social gathering on Shabbat

question, I'd get the answer to "follow the spirit." Being Pentecostal as a child, I had learned what this meant, but it wasn't satisfactory.

I was learning in the Mishnah Walk that the Oral Torah was not simply "men's traditions" but rather an ordained-by-Hashem system of judging cases by Torah throughout Jewish history. I asked one day why we didn't follow the sages. It almost became an argument and that day, I realized they would not be open to learning and changing any further than they had already. I wasn't about to stir up already difficult family situations with a religious debate either. I was on my own.

Not to mention, now that I knew that singing to or worshipping Jesus was idolatry, I stopped singing almost all Christian music. When the worship leader would sing a song of praise to Jesus, I'd get very uncomfortable. There were no crosses – I began looking for them – but there was a model of the Ark of the Covenant. I told the pastor that I was uncomfortable with it, and he said he was too, but it came with the building. I determined that once my obligation was complete for their Sukkot observance, I wasn't going back. I wanted to find a synagogue, but again felt intimidated.

I mentioned earlier that because I chose to observe Shabbat, I lost my marriage. It was my third one. The first two were lost due to abuse issues. They were great losses, but this one was over my spiritual walk, which seemed so strange to me that anyone would divorce for anything less serious than abuse.

My husband was worth over a million dollars, and I had entered the marriage with nothing. I knew I was facing lifetime poverty as I would not be able to earn more than $12-15 per hour in a part-time job at a local retailer and I would have to do so for all my senior years. My retirement annuity wasn't enough to pay the bills for a city apartment and all my expenses. My health had taken a bad turn too, as I couldn't stand for an 8-hour shift anymore.

I wouldn't fight it, because I wouldn't let anything come between me and Hashem. Never again. Each husband had prevented me from going in the direction of Israel for one reason or another, and I thought it my duty to be a submissive wife, with little to no influence on the family decisions. But now, I had the opportunity to go the way of my soul.

During the time I was disengaging from Christianity, I felt abandoned, an emotion I had known since childhood, so it might not be strictly because of what was happening around me. I had no music to sing songs anymore. It could be that all of this was another trigger to my feelings as a young child.

Outside of that, I felt excited. I couldn't stop listening to various rabbis on YouTube or looking up how to do some halacha[4]. I made sure that I learned the various leanings of each rabbi, so I'd know why he was teaching as he was.

Giving up Jesus was no big deal to me as he was a "big brother." My understanding has been fine-tuned, as I never even realized such a thing as replacement theology existed. I always understood Christians to be secondary additions to Israel, so I saw clearly that they are not even that.

Once I understood that the need for the blood sacrifice of Jesus was untrue, and that the Hebrew reads far differently from the English, I was done. I am a decisive person, so I found this quick and easy, once I saw the proof. I was ready to leave as soon as I learned it, without hesitation, but I stayed to fulfill obligations – I felt I needed to keep my word.

I had learned in the Mishnah Walk that the Torah never required remission of sins by means of sacrifice, so I felt great freedom from fear of not having my sins washed away. I also checked out

---

[4] Jewish law

rabbinical teachings on heaven and hell so that I wouldn't be afraid of that anymore. Sure enough, Judaism gave logical teachings on this, especially that Torah doesn't specify details about heaven or hell. I was fine with that as Hashem is good and just. I could definitely trust Him to treat me justly and lovingly.

I think my biggest feeling of detachment was not having anyone to talk to. I am currently in a class with an Orthodox woman teacher and other non-Jewish women. That class helped a lot. I might have gone a completely different direction if I had not had that class.

I live in an area that has about 200 people in total. It is country and the roads don't lead to any cities without many twists and turns. Mainly, farmers live out here, mostly Mennonite Christians who close their shops on Sundays (their Sabbath). I was on my own with or without spirituality, so I had come to terms with that, but I cannot say it was easy to be all alone.

My relationship with Israel has gotten stronger because of this journey. I have always wanted to go to Israel. My first ex-husband, a diplomat, spent four years stationed in Tel Aviv. I asked him if I could come there, but he said it was too dangerous. I'm glad I didn't go, as I would have been all about the Jesus sites. Now I want nothing to do with those. I want to go and see the places that bring the Torah to life.

I joined the Noahide World Center. I took as many free courses as possible and one paid course. I couldn't afford more. The only other Noahide I knew was in another state, at least 100 miles away, and one other friend who wasn't sure if she wanted to remain a Noahide or convert.

The hardest part of this stage was filtering through all the teachings to figure out what a Noahide is, does halachically, and how to live in harmony with like-minded people. That is more difficult than conversion seems to be, as there are no requirements for Noahides to even gather. You are on your own as a Noahide, with no hala-cha. Some say none is allowed. Others say you can do the positive mitzvot.

It just wasn't satisfactory to live in limbo like that. The heart of many Christians is to give God their whole world, their family and their lives. When we see the faulty teachings of Christianity, we can't make that desire go away.

Then, once I decided I needed to convert for the sake of my soul, I couldn't find a way to afford to move, as I was in a very difficult financial situation. There was no way to get to the shul[5] or to afford classes, books, etc.

I found a free course, which made me trust it more, since they would not profit from teaching it. Surely, Hashem will reward the rabbi for opening the doors to those of us who cannot move to con-vert. I understand it may not be accepted in some Jewish synagogues, but at least it's a step in the direction I've longed to go for a long time.

Hashem's faithfulness has been such a rewarding part of this journey! He provided me with a divorce settlement that was first refused to be given, but Hashem changed his mind in a way that was as big as parting the Reed Sea (at least for me). I was able to purchase my home the last week of 2021, in this country town, for less money than I was given. I didn't ask for it; Hashem provided it.

I believe the most important thing is to know your own soul. I can't say I know why Hashem created me, but as I would hear this or that, I'd have a reaction. Sometimes frustration. Other times, excitement. A few times, I sobbed like a baby very loudly. I won-dered why I cry so much. Is it grief over the past losses, abuse and abandonment? Or is it something else?

I am still learning about who I am meant to be. Having children

---

[5] Yiddish for synagogue

kept my mind more on my family. Having a husband since age 17 kept me thinking about him. I didn't think much about myself until I was alone, with no one to talk to. I did a lot of soul searching to figure out why I cry about the beauty of Judaism or the sound of Hebrew or the possibility of not being able to join the congregation.

I am sure it is not an emotional thing per se. It is not an intellectual thing either, as I can talk myself out of a perspective with debate techniques, a strategy I use to check my motives. My only guess is that my soul needs to be connected to the Jewish people in some way.

Honestly, I'll take whatever connection I can get, be it as a Noahide who follows positive commands in Judaism all the way to becoming an Orthodox Jewish woman. I don't deserve such an honor, but my soul craves it. I have no one to please or impress but Hashem.

I've begun studying for conversion. My life is Hashem's to take where it pleases Him. I've fulfilled all my duties to the best of my ability. Now in my senior years, I just want to spend time with Hashem and serve Him by helping others.

In my conversion class, we focus a lot on Micah 6:8. Hashem requires only that we do justice, love mercy, and walk humbly.

I wholeheartedly embrace the heart of Judaism.

If I am able to afford the cost of travel one day, I hope to go to Israel to work on a kibbutz or some other task that would serve the Jewish people. It would be such an honor to do so. I pray that Hashem grant me continued health to be able to do such a thing.

It takes incredible strength to walk this path. It is full of rejection, loss and confusion. I had done much of this throughout my Christian life, so when it came time to question the trinity, the deity of Jesus, and walk away from the last stable thing in my life (my religion) to take the path of loss and rejection, it was a small step for me, though far from easy. I had a lot of emotionally draining days and a lot of days that I studied and researched various ideas.

I retired in 2022 after a terrible bout with COVID and have been rebuilding my health ever since, while also studying Torah. It takes a lot of time, so I don't hurry things. It takes a huge commitment, much like marriage does.

If I am unable to convert, I will follow Judaism as closely as possible with some differences so as not to appropriate the Jewish inheritance, whatever that looks like. Hopefully, many more rabbis will be teaching Noahides in the coming days, as so many long for accurate teaching from Torah scholars and not from non-Hebrew speakers. In the meantime, I learn and attend shul in Nashville, TN.

Deborah lives in the Greater Nashville, Tennessee area and is actively pursuing conversion to Judaism, while living quietly in her country home gardening, building, designing, refinishing furniture, sewing or whatever she finds to do, while enjoying friendships with a new group of friends at Sherith Israel in Nashville and time to research and study the many unresolved questions over the years.

She studied Interior Design at the University of Maryland, worked issuing visas in a couple of embassies in the 1990s while living in Hungary, Indonesia and the Philippines. She did a lot of dressmaking for her daughters, homeschooled her children for 11 years while living abroad, and ran an interior design business, predominantly drafting the design of remodels during her marriage in Nashville. She can be reached at debamyx77@gmail.com.

Giving Up The Idol

Laura Blair

T he first time I asked Jesus to come into my heart, I think I was five years old. I was baptized into the Methodist church after that, and a few years later, into the Baptist church. The Baptist pastor's wife told me to ask Jesus into my heart every day, just to be sure, so I did. As a teenager, I got baptized again by the new pastor in town, who is now my father-in-law. Many years later, I was baptized by someone who pronounced the Sacred Names of the Father, Son, and Holy Spirit as I went under the waters once more. That was the last time, thankfully.

As a child, my mom was the driver of religion in our family. My dad was a good person without need of the church, but he started going to keep the peace. Mom was the neighborhood evangelist. She drove around the area, knocking on doors, asking if the occupant knew that, "God loves you." My two younger siblings and I were left in the car. Every Halloween, we had to pass out Christian tracts while begging for candy.

Each time I got a pimple, my mom would quote the Bible: something about "contention breaketh forth on the skin". She made me feel that God was out to get me for any infraction, so I made sure I sinned big. And then I'd cry and repent, but always feeling guilty, regardless of His grace and unconditional love.

And let's not forget that Jesus was coming back any day! Since I was a straight A student, my teachers wanted me to go to college, but I got married four months after graduating high school, two months after turning 18.

My whole life, all I ever wanted to be was a mother, so my first baby was born 11 months after getting married. I had to beat the rapture deadline! I was in church twice on Sundays, Wednesday night prayer meetings, and Friday night Bible studies. I had a *Strong's Concordance* and no TV. I listened to Christian radio and studied my Scofield Bible.

Recently, I wrote something on Facebook about leaving Christianity, and someone told me that I must not have been a Christian. The person was grateful that God was purging the church of fake believers like myself.

Ironically, I had devoted my whole life to being one.

And I became just like my mom, except worse. I wasn't going to ask people to accept Jesus. I rid myself of all my past friends, and only hung out with Christians. I was judgmental and harsh.

But then I committed adultery. I divorced my husband and the father of my first three children and married the pastor's son. Good thing grace came into play. Good thing the Torah Law didn't apply to me. But I was a wreck. It was as if I had gone crazy, become a totally different person, to do what I did.

A few days after my new marriage, I woke up. I asked my ex-husband and his family for forgiveness. I asked my church for forgiveness. I asked my new husband and my kids for forgiveness. They all graciously extended it to me. But I couldn't accept it. I kept telling myself that I was forgiven, but I didn't feel it at all.

A visiting evangelist told me that I was demon-possessed and suicidal. I had never had a suicidal thought ever, so I started thinking that maybe these guys don't know it all.

I went to the big church in Toronto for "the Father's blessing." Once again, the people praying for me got their prophecy wrong, so I began to wonder. Of course, it must be me though, so I joined the worship team. My husband started Bible college, and he was a small group leader. We were going to work out our "own salvation with fear and trembling" and paying tithes while we ate rice and beans.

Studying for papers for Bible college, my husband, Brian, began to wonder about keeping the Sabbath. Why is there a commandment within the Big Ten that we don't have to keep? The other nine sure get top billing; what about the Sabbath? So, he got involved with chat groups online. He was known int these chat groups by the name Simple Man. My husband is anything but simple; he's an actual genius with much wisdom.

We learned the Name of Israel's God: Yahweh. It made a lot of sense: it's in the Tanach[6] almost 7,000 times.

A family at church invited us to their Passover Seder in 1999, right after the birth of our seventh child. It was amazing! Every element pointed to Jesus/Yeshua(!)

We went to church on Sundays and to Sacred Name assemblies on Sabbaths. We kept our first Feast of Tabernacles in the fall of 2000. That Christmas, things were getting too weird at church. Our kids wanted to be in the nativity play, and we didn't think that was something we should allow. So we left the church, once and for all (the building, not the doctrine).

We started our own Sacred Name Fellowship with two other couples. Over the years, the fellowship grew. Every family was a homeschooling family, like us.

---

[6] Hebrew scripture

Each fall, we would gather with 10-300 other people for the Feast of Tabernacles; traveling or staying local, but always "camping" for the Feast. Those years were exciting. We were learning so many new things, meeting so many "true believers."

Brian and I led the worship team, plus he would teach every other week. We loved it, and they were fun years for our family.

We had met some folks who were pretty hard-line in their understanding of Torah concepts. They threw away all of their kids' dolls. They wouldn't say the days of the week or months of the year. They were ornery in their keeping of the Sabbath, and super strict about clean foods[7].

We weren't like that. Every Friday, we got ready for Shabbat. Music played as we worked. Nothing was too hard, as I had six daughters to help. One of our girls said, "I don't care that we don't have Christmas anymore; we have the Sabbath every week!" No TV on the Sabbath. No computer games. We had fellowship, food and fun.

It lasted about ten years. We were learning things from Jewish websites and books. My husband loved the stories of Rabbi Shlomo Carlebach[8], OBM[9]. Our Pesach[10] seders became more Jewish. Before leading the congregation in song, we led them in the Shema[11]. Every morning, before starting school, I would recite prayers with our children from an Artscroll Siddur[12]. Some of the others in the

---

[7] Avoiding biblically prohibited foods such as pork and shellfish

[8] A well-known rabbi, spiritual leader, composer and singer who passed away in 1994

[9] Of Blessed Memory, a respectful way of referring to someone deceased

[10] Passover

[11] Central Jewish prayer that emphasizes the Oneness of God

[12] Extremely popular version of the Jewish prayerbook

group weren't into Judaism, and men began to preach more of Paul's doctrines each week.

I'm sad to say that things weren't handled well. We all talked too much behind others' backs, and soon enough, there was a split. We started again, with a small group of people meeting in our house every Sabbath.

That Sukkot, we went to South Carolina. We rented a huge house, and three other families and a bachelor joined us. While at a park for lunch, I ran into another Sukkot-keeping group. They had a website. As soon as we were back at the house, I looked them up. They were quite similar in beliefs, and the guy was talking about Yeshua in new ways.

The following year, that group invited me to go to Israel with them! Every Friday night, I had prayed the Ribon Kol ha'Olamim[13] from *The Miracle of the Seventh Day* by Rabbi Adin Steinsaltz[14], OBM. Each time I said, "...have compassion on me in my exile..." I hoped to go to Israel, and I would cry. Finally, I was going!

I won't name the group because they turned out to be a cult, but I went to Israel with them because I didn't know at the time. We were there for two weeks in the Holy Land during Chanukah 2011. I met a Jew for the first time, a man named Hanoch Young. He became a dear friend over the years.

We were in the desert at Biblical Tamar Park for a week. I fell in love with the place. Upon returning home, Brian and I met with Dr. DeWayne Coxon, the man who was managing the park.

In late winter of 2013, I returned to the park with Lydia, one of our daughters, as volunteers. I learned to cook for big groups. Lydia painted the tower, laid the new tile in the British building, and

---

[13] Jewish prayer whose name means Master of all worlds
[14] Popular Chassidic rabbi who passed away in 2020.

cleaned out the cistern and trough. She returned to the park without me the following year. I was back again within two months! That was too hard on the kids, so I did not return until Lydia and I took our husbands in December 2019.

It was Dr. Coxon who told me to read James Tabor's books about Jesus. He was relieved that I was "normal" and he knew about our search for truth. Albeit, he teased me greatly in front of all the Christian volunteers as the "heretic". Those were hard days, as I was not sure yet what Jesus meant to me, and I was alone at the park among very strong Christians.

One pastor at the park, leading a tour of South Africans who were praying for the Arabs, got under my skin, so I returned the favor. He was loud and arrogant, like most pastors I had encountered. He would enter the dining hall singing some praise to Jesus song at the top of his lungs, so I would shut the doors to the kitchen. I was rebuked, and another volunteer there grabbed me and prayed in tongues over me in my ear! That kind of stuff probably kept me from going back, too.

It's hard to say the Shema every day and still think that Jesus/Yeshua is part of the One. It became impossible to continue in the belief that a *man/god died* for my sin(s), that he would have had to die for even one little sin of mine.

I would say something to Brian. He was having an even harder time giving up the idol. I'd cry and pray. He would cry and pray. We were told our whole lives that Jesus was the only way to the Father, and to deny him was the worst sin. Our parents and siblings said we were going to hell, and we were sending our kids there, too.

One of the things I appreciate most about Judaism is the belief that the Satan[15] is not the Christian devil. I grew up very afraid of

---

[15] In Jewish thought, the Satan is the evil inclination that tries to get Jews to sin

demons. I vividly remember one night as a teenager, standing in the kitchen with my mom and a friend. We were all convinced that a ghost was outside the window! We joined hands in prayer and commanded the thing to leave in Jesus' name... but it didn't. The fear was palpable. I finally garnered enough courage to walk over to the window and look at it closer.... it was steam! Oy vey. Haha.

I also read all the Frank Peretti books about spiritual warfare in the heavenly bodies that our prayers fortified. Augh. I don't believe in any of it anymore. There is evil in the world: evil ideas and evil people. And there is YHVH[16]. He is King, and there is no other entity/deity battling with Him over the fate of humankind.

As much as our new lifestyle of keeping the holy days and not eating unclean foods confused our parents, we maintain relationships with them all, thank Yahweh. It's important to us to honor them, as we are commanded, and it is one reason we did not convert.

My dad makes soup every week for family members. He has learned to keep the pork out of ours, but if I couldn't accept his soup because it isn't kosher[17], that would hurt him.

We are blessed with ten kids. The oldest was 16 when we started keeping Shabbat and Feasts. She married a Christian, and they take their kids to church. However, they come to many of our celebrations and are included in everything.

The second born is Jonathan. He married Erin, and they have joined us every step of our journey. In the last few years, they have held bar and bat mitzvah ceremonies for their two oldest children.[18] They probably would have liked to convert. I may have held them

---

[16] An English rendering of one of the Hebrew names of God

[17] Prepared according to the Torah's dietary laws

[18] In the Jewish community, Bar and Bat Mitzvah ceremonies mark the age at which young Jewish people become responsible for their observance of God's commandments

up due to my strong opinions on the synagogues in our city being too left-leaning. We gather together most every Sabbath and Festival. Erin hosts a great party with lots of things for the kids to do.

Our other children also followed us, some for a time. After marrying, though, two have decided that it's silly to believe like we do. One daughter has stopped communicating with us because we "brainwashed" them with our religion. She lives ten minutes away and recently gave birth to our 22nd grandchild, but we aren't allowed to see him.

It's truly heartbreaking, and we pray daily for her heart to soften.

Two other daughters would join more often, but due to little ones and the drive, they don't come every Sabbath. Our two single, youngest kids come often, and are home every Friday night for a special dinner and blessings.

Another family also listened to our questions and the answers we were discovering, so they join us on Sabbaths and Feasts, too. They recently held a bar mitzvah ceremony for their son. We didn't do the bar/bat mitzvah thing with our kids, but it's wonderful to watch these families proclaim their dedication to the Torah and to Yahweh in front of family and friends.

We were blessed to meet the local Chabad rabbi 13 years ago. He was meeting with a small group of Messianics, and we drove an hour north to participate. Then he said that he would love to meet with us in our home! So, for many years, until COVID shut us all in, he would learn with us. Sometimes it was just us, but other times, we'd have 3-5 other couples and kids. We learned about the Rebbe[19], and read some of his books.

---

[19] Rabbi Menachem Mendel Schneerson, the worldwide leader of the Chabad movement who passed away in 1994.

We read Tanya[20], and that was wonderful. The rabbi would always begin with a story, and the kids loved it. We read *The Path of the Righteous Gentile*, and many of us cried! Don't keep the Sabbath!? That can't be right! And it isn't.[21]

The rabbi was perplexed. We have a mezuza[22] on every eligible doorway. He said we shouldn't have them; they are still there. Thankfully, he respected us. At Chanukah parties downtown, he introduces my husband as a righteous gentile so anyone wanting to learn with us would know who to contact. So far, no one has.

We were invited to a party for the rabbi's 3-year-old son; they were cutting his hair for the first time. My husband asked if he could participate. The rabbi took my husband's hand and together they cut a piece of hair. It's amazing how something so honorable can be so humbling.

We almost converted. I set up a meeting with the rabbi of the Conservative synagogue[23] downtown. The day before the meeting, I met Rabbi David Katz on Facebook who was teaching about the Ger[24]. WOW.

We had our meeting with the rabbi, but did not bring up conversion. We went to one Friday night service, which was so foreign that none of us felt comfortable. We continued to learn with the rabbi

---

[20] A foundational work of Chasidic philosophy originally published in 1796

[21] The issue of non-Jews keeping the Sabbath is a complicated matter in Jewish law

[22] A small parchment inscribed with Torah verses and affixed to the doorways of the home

[23] The Conservative movement in Judaism is more liberal on several issues than Orthodox Judaism

[24] Ger toshav is a complex status in Jewish law for non-Jews; it doesn't exist today

teaching about ger toshav. I posted ger stuff on Facebook, but that teacher stopped teaching due to some controversy.

We joined another online group called "United Israel" for a few years, which is led by the author James Tabor. They aren't into the rabbinic stuff, and we learn with a lot of rabbis. They have a few Karaites[25] in the group. Some think they are from a lost tribe. Could be. I haven't thrown out the prophets.

We are members of The Land of Israel Fellowship, which Rabbis Jeremy Gimpel and Ari Abramowitz started at the beginning of the COVID shutdowns. There are a few people like us in the group. Most are Messianics.

Over the years, I've run into the people who say that Jesus never existed; he's myth and legend. Then there are the ones who are so angry about the lies of the church that they call him names and bad-mouth his legacy.

According to the Tabor books, a man named Yehoshua existed and was buried in the Talpiot tomb[26]. It's fascinating really. He married Miriam and they had children. According to some, he was a zealot who died a cruel death at the hands of the Romans. But there were thousands like him. I don't give him a lot of thought these days. *If* he existed, he didn't say all the things attributed to him, nor did he die for the sins of the world.

I finally know the love of Yahweh. He is the only Savior, Redeemer, Creator and King. He is also my Abba[27]. I want to please Him. He longs for me to be the person He designed me to be.

I'm no longer searching for a label to define my beliefs. He wants me to be the best me, with Him along for the ride. Being echad[28]

---

[25] Karaites do not believe in the validity of the Oral Torah

[26] Disputed burial site of Jesus/Yeshua in Jerusalem.

[27] Hebrew for father

[28] Hebrew for one

means more than He is One entity; He is in all that He created, so that's everything, including all that space in a cell that seems unused.

I mentioned a few of our teachers, and there are/were others. We have a few of Rabbi Shalom Arush's[29] books, and a volume of *Likutey Moharan*[30] I saw Rabbi Lazer Brody[31] once. We have several of Rabbi Adin Even Israel Steinsaltz's OBM books and a grandson named after him.

We subscribe to Chabad.org and Aish.com for emails, and I'm learning with a few rabbis on WebYeshiva, as I'm reading daf yomi[32]. I've been a part of Shifra Hendrie's learning about geula[33]. We *love* Rabbi Shlomo Katz[34]. I listen to his classes a few times a week on YouTube. And with Jeremy and Ari's help, he's talking to Rabbi Moshe Weinberger[35] about the non-Jews who are flocking to learn Torah from Zion.

And there was Rabbi Chaim Clorfene[36]. He helped write the book about the Righteous Gentile, then collaborated with Rabbi David Katz (the Ger rabbi) and wrote a book about the Ger. He had much wisdom about things that aren't discussed: the pagan origins of Chanukah, the rabbis vs. the priests and the politics that go on behind rabbinic doors.

As an ex-Christian, I was totally fooled by my pastors and the entire New Testament. When we started learning about Judaism, I was shocked that it has the same issues: too many denominations

---

[29] Israeli rabbi known for popularizing spiritual concepts from Breslov chasidus
[30] Foundational text of Breslov chassidus
[31] Author, life coach and spiritual guide
[32] A daily page of Talmud
[33] Gatesofunity.com
[34] Shiratdavid.com
[35] American Chasidic rabbi, educator, author, translator and speaker
[36] He passed away in 2023.

and sects, men with power who are corrupt, and devotion to a book as old as the NT. Of course, we are told that as non-Jews who can't read Hebrew, we are ignorant and should keep quiet. The Noahide bought that hook, line and sinker.

Of course, thinking for myself gets me in trouble because I'm supposed to honor every rabbi, giving him the devotion due to Moshe Rebbeinu[37]. I cannot. The same brain that questioned the pastors must continue to question the sages, or I am a hypocrite.

I often get the message that, as a non-Jew and a woman, I should shut up. Especially, don't say His Name. It's absolutely maddening. We are heretics to our families and unwanted by the Jews because we say His Name[38], and have some learned opinions. We are told we must toe the line: say "haShem" or "G-d" or "Elokim". We are told to know our place and be satisfied with being a Noahide.

This is why so many avoid the rabbis. But we don't. We know they have much to teach us, so we learn with them and are respectful. Personally, I pray every morning for Yahweh to show up in Zion! Bevakasha Abba[39], teach us Your ways and help us walk in them.

Laura Blair lives in Kalamazoo, Michigan with Brian, her husband of 34 years. Brian owns a business, and Laura is forever the homemaker. They home-educated ten children, including one who is adopted. They have two sons who live at home, including one with special needs. The Blairs have been blessed with 22 grand-children. Laura can be reached at blairfam10@sbcglobal.net.

---

[37] Moses our teacher

[38] The Jewish custom is to avoid using any of God's names except in prayer. It is connected to a Jewish interpretation of the Third Commendment.

[39] Hebrew for "Please Father"

The Anguish In My Questions

Andrea Chester

EDITOR'S NOTE: *Andrea routinely capitalizes words that refer to God. About this custom, she explained, "GOD isn't just a person, HE is the primary person. To me, it signifies HIS importance in my life."*

About 25 years ago, I faced a crisis of faith. My sister, who had always been able to think outside the box, asked me a question that threw my neatly arranged religious concepts into total disarray. I had to scramble for answers to questions I had never asked before. And, because my faith was one of the most crucial elements of my identity, I knew that whatever I found out, it would change who and what I was.

First of all, I had to reflect on what I had always believed. I was reared in a rather ordinary Christian home, with GOD alone as the very core of my faith. Somehow, I never completely anchored my belief system in Jesus, and never thought him equal with GOD. I considered him to be vastly more than an ordinary human, but I struggled with how to define more.

In college, I migrated from the staid worship services of my youth in the Methodist church to the joyous, praise-filled worship services of the Charismatic movement. It felt warm, the way I imagined worship *should* feel. I thought I had come home, but it was just a stop-over in the journey.

When my children were young, I started watching Herbert W. Armstrong and his son, Garner Ted Armstrong. They had some insights I'd never encountered before. I learned that the Sabbath and the Jewish Festivals had some present applications to me, a non-Jew.

I attended the Church of GOD International for several years. From there, it was just a short step to Messianic Judaism, but questions were beginning to bubble up to the surface of my mind. By that point, although Jesus was still an important figure in my faith, I was beginning to wonder just where he was supposed to fit. That's when my sister asked me a simple question: "What would it do to my faith if Jesus was only a man?"

At first, I was aghast. What could she be saying? He was Messiah! He had died for my sins. No ordinary man would, or could, do that! I shoved those pesky little doubts into the dusty recesses of my thoughts, but they wouldn't stay there.

Where could I look for unbiased answers? My understanding of Jesus was entirely from a New Testament standard. I knew that pastors and Christian theologians would point me towards the traditionally used Old Testament prophecies, proof texts about his birth and death like Isaiah 6 and Isaiah 53.

Suddenly, that wasn't acceptable to me. For example, why would Isaiah tell King Ahaz about a child to be born several hundred years in the future? It didn't fit anymore.

Then, it occurred to me.

I had known several Jewish people while I was growing up, but my personal experience with Judaism was in Messianic synagogues. Everything I knew included the Jesus factor. I had never asked a religious Jew why he didn't believe.

Through the marvels of the Internet, I found an orthodox Jew in Michigan and an orthodox rabbinic student in Monsey, New York, and asked them for some answers. Bless their generous souls; they must have sensed the anguish in my questions, because they helped me re-examine familiar biblical concepts without the Christological focus.

I learned about basic discrepancies between what the Hebrew Scriptures said about GOD and what the New Testament said about Jesus. After all, if he was the Jewish Messiah, he had to fit the description. He had to *fulfill* the description, but there were also many things he *didn't* have to be. He didn't have to be divine. He didn't have to be sinless. And, very interestingly, nowhere in Tanach[40] does it mention that he would be a miracle worker. Funny, that seemed to be Jesus' main claim to fame.

Note: Many common religious themes are pagan in origin. See if you recognize these scenarios. A human virgin gives birth to the child of a god whose destiny is to redeem mankind. The redemption requires the bloody death of this sinless human/god hybrid. However, most of those for whom this sacrifice is offered don't even recognize what's happening, making it even more poignant and unfair. The redeemer's followers commemorate his life and death by eating a special meal, including the mystic elements of his body and his blood. (Big no-no there. Eating/drinking blood and human sacrifice are explicitly forbidden in the Torah, and human flesh is *not* kosher!) In many pagan myths, the savior is resurrected from the dead.

I do think that the real Jesus was a Torah-observant Jew who taught his followers deep Torah truth using parables. I think the religion that grew up around his legend has been revised many times since his murder on a Roman cross. A wonderful resource

---

[40] Hebrew scriptures

for more information is Jews for Judaism[41], especially with Rabbi Michael Skobac.

My mentors guided me through dozens of Scriptures that I'd always viewed from a Christian perspective. Taken in their original context, they didn't say what I'd always been taught they did. It was like jetting between a foreign country and my own, day after day. Jet lag set in, making me feel disoriented, frustrated, and as though I didn't really belong anywhere. Eventually, I found out that I did belong somewhere.

So, who and what am I? I am bas Noah[42]. Bnei Noah[43] dates back to the time of Adam and Eve. There's a lot of confusion about us and, unfortunately, some hostile curiosity.

Right now, we're a loosely connected group of people who believe in the one true GOD. Although our numbers are growing, there aren't many congregations of us. We recognize that humans are directly responsible to the Creator, without the need of a mediator. We are not Christians, we aren't Jews, and we're not a cult. Our name comes from the Hebrew for Children of Noah. We acknowledge Torah's primacy, and long for the appearance of Moshiach[44].

What do we believe? There are seven universal laws mandated for all humans. They're the foundation for any other system of laws in the Bible, including the Ten Commandments. The seven divine decrees are:

1. Do not worship idols. (This includes ascribing GOD-hood to a human or adopting pagan customs to worship Him. This is the one command that many religions transgress without even knowing it.)

---

[41] Jewsforjudaism.org
[42] Hebrew for daughter of Noah, a Noahide
[43] Hebrew for Children of Noah
[44] Hebrew for messiah

2. Do not blaspheme the Name of GOD.
3. Do not murder.
4. Do not have forbidden sexual alliances. (Incest, rape and adultery are all prohibited. Homosexual behavior is also forbidden.)
5. Do not steal.
6. Do not eat the limb of a still-living animal. (The modern application of this is don't mistreat animals.)
7. Establish courts of justice.

Many of us are still struggling with how to integrate these truths into the framework of our lives and families. Many of us still live in predominantly Christian families, and we aren't sure how to handle holidays and the questions of our loved ones. Relax. GOD is in charge. The first, most important, step is realizing that Jesus isn't GOD.

How do Bnei Noah fit into traditional Judaism? With all respect, from my understanding, traditional Judaism actually fits into Bnei Noah, not the other way around. Oddly enough, most Jews know little about us, and view us with a mixture of suspicion and amused tolerance.

Mosaic law is built on the Bnei Noah foundation, with additional commandments distinguishing Jews from the rest of the world. A peculiar nation, Jews are the priesthood and the rest of humanity is the general congregation. We're all necessary to the ordained function of society.

GOD'S original code was given in Adam's day, and reiterated right after the Flood, as evidenced by the name, children of Noah. All three great monotheistic religions had their beginnings in us; Abraham was a ben Noah[45].

---

[45] Hebrew for son of Noah

How do religious Christians view Bnei Noah? Most Christians don't know we exist. Others consider us traitors, turning our backs on GOD'S salvation. However, more Christians are beginning to recognize that most of the claims about Jesus don't fit Torah. Notice, I said claims about him, not the claims he made. It's hard to be certain about what he did or didn't say, since it was 2000 years ago.

Why become Bnei Noah? Because I cannot, in good faith, worship as a Christian any longer. I believe I am as much GOD'S daughter as Jesus was HIS son. I think he was a good man, whose teachings and sayings have been perverted and twisted for various purposes. I no longer accept the murder of that young Jewish man, 2000 years ago, on a Roman cross, as the substitutionary death for my sins. I earnestly believe that each of us will stand before the Throne of Judgment to answer for ourselves, not with Jesus as our proxy.

There's some excellent moral teaching in the New Testament, but there's also a strong anti-Jewish flavor in places. I now regard it as a commentary, but not the infallible, fully inspired Word of GOD. Unfortunately, there's proof that many NT passages have been changed and re-written several times. Those changes cannot be explained away as mere translation errors. Many former Christians choose to disregard the New Testament entirely. (As one rabbi put it, Jesus has become irrelevant to my way of worship.)

Why not convert to Judaism? The righteous of all nations have a share in Heaven. There's no need to convert to Judaism.

Now, back to who this Bas Noah is. I still struggle with how to apply what I'm learning. In some ways, I guess I'll always speak with a Christian accent. Listen to me for a while, and you can tell from whence I came.

Perhaps the most profound effect of disengaging from traditional Christianity, for me, is that I no longer feel the closeness, the familiarity of GOD that I had as a Christian. I lost the human face, the feeling that HE could identify with me in the same way that I can identify with another person. While I never believed that Jesus was GOD, he represented, to me, someone who knew me through and through. It helped me understand GOD as the FATHER, the CREATOR, because Jesus was HIS Son. I guess he kind of represented GOD'S spokesperson. The best way I can explain that to a religious Jew is to say Jesus was, to me, what Moses is to them.

I'm grateful to all those who taught and prodded and challenged me to think and grow in my Bible knowledge. My grandmothers and my parents taught me a strong, valid system of morals and values, and a reverent love for the GOD of Abraham, Isaac, and Jacob. My sister's thoughtful question sent me searching for ever-deepening answers. I don't regret that I was a Christian, but I have learned why I can't be one any longer.

I no longer depend on a man-made structure to support my worship of GOD. Torah is my text, and observant Jews are my trusted teachers. I'm not sure who Jesus was, but it isn't very important to me any longer. Because of him, many non-Jewish people believe in God and long for Moshiach, so he did whatever GOD put him in the world to do. (In fact, the great rabbi and scholar, Maimonides[46] himself, said that.) I don't discuss religion with people anymore. I speak freely about GOD, but not religion.

Sometimes, I feel quite lonely in this adventure. My sister, who became a full-fledged Jew, died seven years ago. My mother was firmly bas Noah the last few years of her life. My children are still in various stages of Christianity, and my husband doesn't talk about the things of GOD very much. Sometimes, there's just no substitute for grabbing a cup of coffee and a danish and sitting down to talk things

---

[46] Also known as the Rambam, Maimonides, who lived in the 12th c., is one of the most influential Torah scholars of all time

out! I live in the beautiful mountains of western North Carolina, not exactly a hotbed of Jewish community.

Thank GOD for the Internet! I have learned a great deal from Aish haTorah, Ask Noah, Jews for Judaism, and from several books. One of the best, clearest, and most comprehensive of those books is Michael Dallen's *The Rainbow Covenant*. I now have several very dear Orthodox Jewish friends, but most of them are solely online.

As GOD brings us closer to the time of Moshiach, there will be more and more righteous gentiles learning about true worship, unlearning unacceptable practices. We, in this generation, are watching an exciting chapter of history unfold. May we see redemption speedily, and in our time.

> *Andrea Chester lives in the mountains of western North Carolina with her husband, a dog, and a cat. They have a son and three daughters, who have given them the joy of seven grandchildren and three great-granddaughters. Her favorite hobbies include reading, writing and crocheting. She has been learning Torah on some level for most of her life. Andrea can be reached at tinachester@hotmail.com.*

Read Your Bible

Ada Davis

Both my parents were Presbyterian, but by the time I came on the scene, they were not attending church. Dad died when I was six years old and my mother raised me. There was no religious instruction that I can remember, but nighttime prayers were said and Mum's constant quote was, "All you may need, He will provide." Somehow, she managed to instill in me the understanding that my father was in heaven and I had a Father in heaven, and there was a difference.

Her other message was, "If you are ever in trouble, Ada, read your Bible." But that advice came with instructions. Ignore the Old Testament. It's just history. All you need to study are the first four gospels. After that, it gets weird and those things were only for back then anyway.

Well, with instructions like that, what could possibly go wrong?!

Did I have a Bible? Maybe.

Did I hit trouble? Absolutely.

As it says in the song "To Life! (L'Chaim!)" from *Fiddler on the Roof,* "Our great men have written words of wisdom to be used when hardship must be faced. Life obliges us with hardship, so the words of wisdom shouldn't go to waste."

In 1978, I asked a friend at work to ask her mother what I should get as a first Bible. She pointed me to *Good News for Modern Man*. It had color photographs of Israel and I loved it.

I read the four gospels and wanted more. I can still remember the sense of trepidation as I turned the last page of John and ventured into the Acts of the Apostles. I was hooked.

In the Gospel of Matthew, I read "as in the days of Noah," and I understood that to mean during the time of the flood. Matthew wrote about how, just as in the days of Noah, people would ignore the warning of the coming disaster and carry on as normal.

As I dove into the other books, I was fascinated.

But then came Hazon (Revelation). Wow! I discovered things that riveted me and would never leave my heart.

Addressing the community at Ephesus in Revelation 2:6, Jesus said, "Yet this you have, that you hate the works of the Nikolaites, which I also hate." I wanted to know who the Nikolaites were.

Speaking to the folks at Pergamos in Revelation 2:14, Jesus said, "But I hold a few matters against you, because you have those who adhere to the teaching of Bil'am, who taught Balaq to put a stumbling block before the children of Yisra'el, to eat food offered to idols, and to commit whoring."

I had to find out what that was about. I needed to know more about the seven Spirits of Elohim[47] from Revelation 3:1, too. And so began an adventure back into the history of the Old Testament to discover the roots of faith and its guidelines.

All was good until I encountered a train of thought that didn't fit with what I read in Scripture. Talk of a rapture and we as "Christians" (I just cringe at the word nowadays) escaping the tribulation. The

---

[47] One of several ways of referring to God in Hebrew

theory was that the wrath of HaShem[48], poured out in the tribulation was reserved for the Jews, and we were spared that.

I couldn't stomach it. It wasn't fair. The Jews had suffered so much through all the ages. Why again? I remember I asked HaShem one night, "If there should be a choice, I'd rather stay and walk through this with them!"

My life ticked on. In 1986, I had the chance to visit Israel, and my heart melted. I stood on the Mount of Olives in tears and just wanted to become those tears, that I might soak into the ground.

When I returned to New Zealand, anytime I read or heard *Jerusalem* my eyes glazed over, and I couldn't function. That went on for months. Today, I know it to be that longing for Israel that never ceases.

However, my first husband was failing in health. It was the beginning of a 13-year battle with emphysema. In 1997, Brent had a lung transplant and ultimately died in 1998 from organ rejection. I had no time to contemplate the importance of Israel and Jerusalem in my heart.

Father comforted me and covered me, then one day, I spat the dummy[49]. I felt He was pulling me along too fast. I stopped and I stomped my foot in the dust and said, "You don't understand. My teddy bear is broken, and you are taking me too fast," as I pointed to a teddy, broken and dusty on the side of the road.

Immediately, my heart pinged, and I asked, "Oh, Father! What is Your teddy bear?" He continued to insist I move on, but eventually, He showed me His teddy bear, His brokenness over His people, who are called to serve Him, who have fallen away from HIS righteous

---

[48] Hebrew for "The Name" and a way to refer to God without using a sacred name

[49] Australian slang meaning to lose control of one's temper

path, falling into the trap of doing life and not seeking to honour Him in everything. Time and time again, we have been wayward, and He has rebuked and turned us back, yet still, we turn away.

Early in 1999, the church I attended decided they had two loose ends in the form of two mature single people that they needed to tidy up. Evan had been widowed the year before me. By the beginning of 2000, Father had lifted the blinkers off our eyes and we were married.

Thanks again to *Fiddler on the Roof,* I always knew that if I should marry again, I wanted a canopy[50]. Trying to explain to a Pentecostal pastor that we believed we were, in fact, converted to the God of Abraham, Isaac and Jacob was an interesting experience. However, he played the game and we have a bag of broken glass to prove it![51]

Now in a like-minded union, Scripture really began to open up. We had both been Revelation and Tanach[52] readers way before, but now it began to blossom. While our faith was strong, there was a nagging doubt that something really significant was missing.

Around 2004, I read an article in a women's magazine about the pagan roots of Christmas! We sometimes tend to just accept what we have always known without question. It's when we question that truth is revealed. Rapidly we discovered "our fathers had inherited lies"[53] and there was no going back. Christmas and Easter we axed.

That cost us our family.

In 2010, we were reading Exodus one morning and looked at

---

[50] A reference to a chuppah under which Jewish couples marry

[51] A reference to the glass that is broken at the end of a Jewish wedding, symbolizing the destruction of Jerusalem

[52] Hebrew scripture

[53] Jeremiah 16:19

each other and said, "We're not keeping the Ten Commandments, namely #4."[54]

That cost us our fellowship and friends.

The layers began to lift off. The next challenge we took on was clean food. But I had a problem. We had given a sheep to a friend and he gave us a pig. Our sheep went off cleaned and dressed in cheesecloth and we had to collect a *live* pig!

We brought Mr. P home, plopped him in the stock pens and Evan said to me, "Do not feed that pig!" Over the next six hours, I checked on the pig. The pig looked up at me, expecting food. The pig seemed to be asking me, "Oh, what you got for me? Apples, yum. What you got for me? Bread, yum. What you got for me?"

When morning came, so did the man with the gun. Mr. P looked up and asked, "Oh! What you got for... BANG!" Because I had been feeding him, when the bullet came, he still thought he was getting treats and he had no fear. I have often said, in the slaughter of an animal, it should know nothing, but it will break the man's heart.

He became the happiest dead pig in history. Except now we had a *dead* pig.

It wasn't long after that we were reading the clean foods list. With a dead pig in the freezer, I needed to understand why he was out of bounds. Finally, the answer seeped through. Because God said so.

We buried Mr. P.

The next issue HaShem handled for me was Bluff oysters. I had grown up in Dunedin, about three hours from Bluff. I grew up with Bluff oysters and hadn't given them any thought at all in this new equation. We now lived in the north of New Zealand and they weren't on our agenda anymore. But one day, driving to town,

---

[54] The commandment to keep the Sabbath

an advertisement came on the radio for the local Bay of Islands Oyster Festival. Immediately, I felt sick in the stomach, and blessed HaShem for the transition to clean foods.

We listened to podcasts occasionally and encountered vastly differing ideas. In 2012, we discovered the Noahide Laws. Ultimately, this was not for us; we adhered to the Ten Commandments.

But I grasped one of the Noahide Laws with both hands and all my heart, a law I understood to mean that we must cut nothing off a living creature.[55] We are sheep farmers, and one practice I was never happy with was docking[56]. Now I knew why and now I had a valid reason. All little lambs kept their tails and boys grew up entire[57].

For us, leaving Christianity was not all smooth. The leaving bit was simple. We walked away and called ourselves the "Be-Leavers."

The extraction of beliefs and teaching was trickier.

We still, and I think always will, check whether or not He really said something we thought. The discoveries were precious, but we had fallen for lies before. Now we needed it in black and white.

It was lonely. Again, words from "I Have Decided To Follow Jesus," a song from the 1980s, held us. "Should none go with us, still we will follow." It stands even better today in this Torah walk, for surely few come with us.

Eventually, it came down to believing that "our fathers had inherited lies." Pagan elements had woven their way through the storytelling and we wanted none of it. To test the point, one night, I took my granddaughters to the ballet in the town hall. As we were waiting to enter, they told me this was where they went to church.

My heart pinged with a longing for fellowship, for music, for

---

[55] Technically, the law prohibits eating the limb of an animal that is still alive.
[56] Surgically shortening the tail of an animal.
[57] Without being castrated

robust lung-wrenching singing outside the shower. It hit me hard. I stood there asking Father, "Could I just go once? One time?" I knew it wasn't wise, but the answer came days later when I read, "You can't get out of the church till you get the church out of you."

Settled, doors shut.

Only one of our family came down this path with us. My eldest step-daughter in Melbourne had said for years, "There must be something else!" The three of us would shake our heads and want more, but she came along on her own, discovering the treasure that we had discovered separately, which made it even more precious.

Today, Evan and I are in loose contact with several Orthodox Jews inside Israel, most of whom we discovered after October 7. One treasure is a man who stopped us on Jaffa Road in Jerusalem in 2016. We started talking and he asked if we were Jewish. My only answer to that was to tap my wrist and say, "We can't prove the blood, but it's something inside." His words to us have been cement. He looked up and said, "You don't have to. HaShem knows."

It became our glue, a confirmation, that a rabbi on Jaffa Road understood this weird floundering dilemma we live. "Something" that we cannot control runs within us, and leaps in the presence of His people and in His Word. It was as though Hashem smiled on us and said, "You belong." It was one of those precious things that can't be taken from you.

We have a tiny community of like-minded people in New Zealand. Our fractured local group meets every two months. The diversity of understanding on issues ranging from calendars, months and Sabbaths is almost distressing; you put six people in a room and get 29 opinions.

But we are all we have in a fallen society, and we all keep a kind of kosher – "Kiwi Kosher," meaning we do our very best in a filthy world to eat biblically clean. We scour ingredients, eat our own home-kill (blood drained and buried) and avoid things like red food colouring.

We try to keep an eye on each other for safety. The New Zealand Torah community has been damaged by a crafty scam and become even more fractured. We are not so open now to folks who seem to say the right words.

Today, we believe we are part of the ingathering, yet my original request of HaShem still remains and we'll stay behind and help them through the gate if it comes to that.

While we believe we would merit to be part of the ingathering if we could prove the blood, we know we have a post out here in the diaspora. It's the "not all prisoners of war have come home"[58] instinct.

Too many are still stuck in church, others will be caught in the last days tribulation and we believe we have a post to serve them and show them their Elohim, to guide hearts back to Torah. We also believe many will come out of Israel and need redirection to find their way home (to HaShem). We long for Israel, for Yerushalayim[59], but we still believe we have a duty here.

These precious days are full of deception and danger, yet in Yah[60] we trust. May He provide and guide.

Evan and Ada Davis are Kiwis who have lived and worked in New Zealand all their lives, escaping occasionally to visit Australia, Canada, UK and Israel. Both widowed in the late 1990s, they found new life together at the turn of the century.

---

[58] From the song "It Is Finished" by Bill & Gloria Gaither

[59] Jerusalem

[60] A shortened form of one of the Hebrew names for God used primarily by people involved with Hebrew Roots

Evan is an engineer by trade and Ada has worked in retail, insurance and banking. Both now retired, they just can't help fiddling with something. They shepherd a little stud flock of South Suffolk sheep, ran an Airbnb accommodation before there was an Airbnb, and invented a series of party plates to hold food and beverages, making networking a little easier, until New Zealand banned single-use plastics! Their latest venture has been to subdivide the farm into residential lifestyle blocks and above all, they would love to see that become a moshav[61]-style, Torah-observant settlement.

Both began to awaken to Torah in 2004 when they began to recognise the pagan influences in the only religion they had known. They began keeping Shabbat in 2014. Ada can be reached at skikiwinz@gmail.com.

---

[61] Cooperative agricultural community in Israel

The Unfinished Journey: Leaving Christianity, Finding Judaism

Ginni Gamble

"We don't eat pork because the Bible tells us not to." This is the simple yet profound statement that started our now almost five-year journey out of Christianity and into Judaism.

Our daughters had been playing with two new friends who made this statement, causing them to come running to us, exclaiming with quizzical looks, "But we eat pork and we believe in the Bible!" At that moment, my husband John and I knew where this was headed.

Several years prior, dear friends had explained to us how they had been studying that the Torah had not been done away with, and, in fact, was still very much relevant today. So, John and I knew it was time to dig into what we believed and why we believed it.

We went to the story in the New Testament book of Acts about how Peter had seen a vision of a sheet coming down with both clean and unclean animals together and God had said, "Rise Peter, kill, and eat." In Mark 7:19, Jesus declared all foods to be clean. We explained to our girls that this meant we could now eat all things and sent them on their way, pleased with ourselves for arming them with the truth.

But as time went on, I didn't feel settled in my answer, and neither did John. It was as if God was saying, "Are you sure about that? Are you sure about the answer you gave your daughters?" So we decided to dig in more and really research the meaning behind Peter's vision and Jesus's words in Mark.

That decision led to countless hours of intense study. We looked up scripture, watched YouTube videos, read blog posts and articles, consumed everything we could on the topic and on both sides of the issue. Had the Torah really been done away with or not?

It came to a point in our research that I was so confused and overwhelmed. I didn't know what was true and only wanted to serve and please God. So I prayed one of the most earnest, heartfelt prayers of my life, "God please show me what is true! Whatever it is I will do it! If Christianity is correct, I will stay in Christianity, but if your Torah is correct and still valid for today, then I will give up Christianity and start walking in Your ways." After that prayer, I felt like a huge weight had been lifted from me and lightbulbs of understanding began to come on.

Our journey had begun.

At that time, John and I were both very active members in our Southern Baptist church in North Texas. We had both been raised in church and "saved" from very early ages. John taught our Sunday School class and sang on the praise team, while I helped with women's ministry events and occasionally taught the children's service.

The Baptist church uses the *Baptist Quarterly*, a book with pre-selected lessons for the Sunday School teachers to teach from. I remember vividly my husband's exasperated groan when he saw what he would teach for the next quarter. "Numbers and Deuteronomy?!"

he exclaimed. "I don't know anything about these Old Testament books. How am I supposed to teach them?"

But as any teacher knows, the best studying comes from preparing to teach someone else, and that is exactly what happened. God used that time in John's life to really open up his eyes to the truth and the everlasting nature of His Torah. He saw it from a fresh perspective and ended up really enjoying those lessons.

Then COVID hit, and our church, like thousands of others, shut its doors. Once it was time to reopen, John and I knew we couldn't go back. By that time, we had studied so much that we knew, without a doubt, that Jesus had not done away with the Torah, and that since we had been brought into the Covenant through Christ (as was our understanding at that time), we were obligated to keep it.

We could no longer teach or participate in a church that taught otherwise, nor could we participate in Christmas or Easter services. It was time to have a meeting with our pastor.

The meeting, thankfully, went well. Our pastor listened patiently as we explained our newfound knowledge and convictions. When we had finished he told us he could see how passionate we were and that this was just a little "bump in our journey" and who knows, John might come back as a pastor one day! Little did he know this so-called "bump" was, in fact, a completely new path and we had just barely taken our first steps.

Not long after this meeting, John and I decided we needed to move, and not just to another city, but to Arkansas, an entirely different state. Although we felt a pull to relocate for several reasons, it brought about unintended heartbreak for our local extended family. We would later find that this decision to move away gave us a lot of space to begin walking in our new understanding of keeping Torah and we grew by leaps and bounds.

When we arrived in our new home, we knew no one there. It

felt lonely and we craved community. Not long after, however, we were connected with some local families who also kept Torah. We were thankful to get plugged into a group of like-minded believers.

Over time, differences in calendars, the shape of the Earth, eschatological views like Preterism[62], and many other inconsequential topics began to fracture our local community. Sub-groups split off and none of them were thriving.

By this time, we had found online teachers, namely Rico Cortes and later Joseph (Joe) Good, who taught Torah from a more Jewish perspective and our hearts and souls were drawn to the wisdom found in Judaism. Joe also taught extensively on the Temple, helping us understand the offerings, the Temple protocols, and the overall significance of the Temple in Jewish life. Through his research and teaching, we grew to love the Temple and anxiously await the day when the Third Temple will be rebuilt!

Thankfully, Hashem[63] led us to another local family that also loved the Jewish people and their traditions, and we began studying alongside them. However, our families began to feel very isolated. Although we were in a sea of Torah keepers, the majority didn't love the Jews and disagreed with our more Jewish observances.

As things in our spiritual life changed, the dynamics of our relationship with our families also changed. My parents, who are strong Christian believers, active in their local Baptist church, have always been the ones John and I would go to when we had a Biblical question. We would often have deep and engaging spiritual discussions with them.

All that changed when we told them the Torah had not been

---

[62] A Christian eschatological view that teaches some Biblical prophecies as if they have already happened.

[63] Literally, The Name. A Jewish way to refer to God without risking using God's name in vain.

done away with, that we were keeping Shabbat and no longer celebrating Christmas and Easter. It was like a gut punch to their soul. Our once thriving dialogue has become surface-level at best. They no longer want to discuss anything Biblical with us. There is this constant elephant in the room and it is palpable every time we are with them.

I will never forget the first Christmas we weren't there. I felt awful. Not because I wanted to celebrate. I did not. But I am an only child and my two daughters are their only grandchildren. Without us, they would be celebrating alone. This hurt my soul.

As for John's family, who are also very active in their local Baptist church, we almost never discussed spiritual matters with them. But once we began keeping aspects of the Torah, it opened up a lot of dialogue between us, more than we had ever had before. Almost every visit with them led to a spiritual discussion. They disagreed with us, and some of those first discussions were a bit heated, but eventually, we were able to share all that we had been learning.

They still disagree, but they have been willing to listen and still ask questions. John's mom has been kind enough to try to understand our new dietary requirements and cook things that we can eat, which has been very thoughtful and greatly appreciated. For the last several years they have invited my parents over to spend Easter with them. It did my heart good to know my parents were not spending another holiday alone.

As one chapter closes, another opens and it was time for our family to close our chapter in Arkansas and move back to Texas. There were several reasons for this decision, but one was to be closer to family. We knew we did not want to move back to the congested Dallas area where we are originally from, but we felt drawn to a slower life in East Texas. This allowed us to be about two hours away from family and able to visit them much more often.

Our families were excited to have us closer, but now it was our best friends' turn to be devastated as we moved away. Trust me, we made our best effort to get them to move to Texas with us, but their journey is their own, and Hashem has mighty things in store for them in their next chapter as well. We are still very close and visit each other as often as possible.

There were no shuls[64] near us in Arkansas, but in our area there are two, a Conservative and a Reform. By this time, we had furthered our journey towards Judaism, even learning more about the daily prayers in the siddur[65], and we wanted to visit a synagogue. But would they let a family of non-Jews come?

We had a friend in town who knew the rabbi at the Conservative shul, and he introduced us. John had a nice phone call with him explaining our journey and why we wanted to visit. The rabbi put our family's name on the list to be let into shul that coming Shabbat.

We were so excited and nervous! What should we wear? Does my head need to be covered? How about John? Can he wear a kippah as a non-Jew, or would that be offensive? What should we say or not say? Would they be welcoming or standoffish? I had no idea what to expect.

I thought my heart had sunk into my stomach as we walked in the doors the first time. We knew no one. Thankfully, a man greeted us, showed us where to get a siddur and Tanach[66] off the shelf and where to sit in the sanctuary. The rabbi came in and introduced himself and then service began. It was beautiful! Almost all done in Hebrew, but the siddur had English on one side that helped us

---

[64] synagogues

[65] Jewish prayerbook

[66] Hebrew scriptures

follow along, as there were many Hebrew words we recognized and could pick out.

When it came time for the Ark[67] to be opened and the Torah scroll to come out, my heart was unprepared for what happened. As the Torah scroll was paraded around the room and we were singing and reaching out to touch it with our siddurim[68], tears just began flowing from my eyes. I couldn't stop them. Never in my life had I seen a Torah scroll in person, and so elaborately decorated. I caught several glances from others, probably wondering why I was so emotional. It took quite some time to compose myself, but I finally made it through the rest of the service.

Afterward, we were invited to stay at Oneg[69]. Several people introduced themselves, even inviting us to join them at someone's home later that evening. We decided to go and were thankful we did, as we made many new friends that night.

After that first visit, we never missed a week. We continued meeting with our new Jewish friends every Friday evening in someone's home for Erev Shabbat[70], and then went to shul for Shabbat services. We learned a lot!

It was through these gatherings in people's homes on Erev Shabbat that we first started questioning the validity of Jesus. You see, up until that point, even though we were walking closer to Judaism, we still believed Jesus was the messiah. Along the way, we had realized he was not God, and that the virgin birth was not real, but we still believed he was messiah.

---

[67] The designated place for Torah scrolls in the synagogue

[68] Hebrew for Jewish prayerbooks (plural)

[69] Informal social gathering on Shabbat after prayer services, generally involving refreshments. In Orthodox shuls, this gathering is usually referred to as a kiddush.

[70] The preparatory hours just before Shabbat begins

There have been moments all throughout our journey that really stick out in my mind - moments that were major shifts in our understanding. One of these moments occurred as we were about to leave one night. The topic of Jesus not being messiah came up and one of the men stated that Jesus did not fulfill any of the messianic prophecies in Tanach.

I was floored. He continued sharing three or four examples and said there were ten in total. We had not shared with anyone that we still believed Jesus was messiah because we didn't want to be rejected and turned away. This Jewish man had no clue the massive door he had just unlocked for us.

Jesus didn't fulfill any of the messianic prophecies in Tanach? How could this be? We had to dig in. We watched several videos from Rabbi Tovia Singer and other rabbis who explained what these ten requirements for messiah were. One by one, we went through the list and found he was right. Jesus had not fulfilled them. We also began to understand that salvation doesn't come from a man, but from Hashem alone, and that no man could die to provide forgiveness for the sins of others.

We continued studying and purchased *Kosher Jesus* and *The Mythmaker* which furthered our understanding of who Jesus really was and how it was Paul who really inspired Christianity and made claims to Jesus's messiahship. This was the final straw.

You can walk so far away from Christianity, but you haven't truly left until you let go of Jesus.

At times, the newfound knowledge was freeing. Finally, things that never quite made sense could be understood with such clarity. Yet it was also scary and upsetting. You see, the theology of Christianity was like a massive building, crumbling down all around us. It was so hard to watch the building blocks of our faith falling one by one. It was an unsettling sensation and it rattled us to our core. And yet, this demolition was necessary to rebuild our faith from the ground up.

Letting go of Jesus was the last piece. The final stone had fallen.

There are times I greatly miss being a part of the church. I miss being involved in ministries and serving others. I miss attending ladies' events and Bible studies. I miss singing together in corporate worship to God. I miss the children's and teen's activities my daughters could participate in.

We have nothing like that now, and it's definitely a gaping hole within our spiritual life. But one thing that has helped has been joining a small study group of non-Jewish women, led by a Jewish woman. When I was invited, I jumped at the chance to learn from a rebbetzin living in Israel! What a special treat it has been! She has taught me so much from the storehouses of wisdom within Judaism.

When you leave Christianity, you have a lot of theological and doctrinal baggage you carry with you. Some are quickly and easily shed, but some are so deeply ingrained that it takes time to uproot. Learning from a Jewish woman has helped in the process of uprooting some of the Christian ideas and concepts I still have within me and replacing them with the Jewish understanding. I have a long way to go in this endeavor, but I am so thankful Hashem has brought me such a patient, knowledgeable and dedicated teacher who tempers her teachings with sensitivity to our Christian backgrounds.

I strongly encourage anyone coming out of Christianity to find a trustworthy Jewish teacher and mentor to assist in your journey. Not only are they a valuable wealth of knowledge, but they can help you avoid the pitfalls of studying Torah and Torah concepts on your own.

I have seen firsthand the damage that can be done when one comes out of Christianity, wanting to serve Hashem, but not learning from Jews. Eventually, they come up with their own strange views and doctrines, unusual calendars and traditions, even teetering on the edge of starting their own cult. It is disastrous.

There is much wisdom found in Zechariah 8:23, *"Thus said the LORD of Hosts: In those days, ten men from nations of every tongue will take hold — they will take hold of every Jew by a corner of his cloak and say, 'Let us go with you, for we have heard that God is with you.'"*

We were so grateful to be able to attach ourselves to the Jewish people at our local shul. However, things at the shul took a turn when an unfortunate and disruptive event occurred. The event outraged many of the families and they ultimately left the shul. We ended up deciding to leave as well. Thankfully these same families still met every Erev Shabbat, and then gathered again for Shabbat day. Sadly, there were some things going on in this group that we did not agree with and after a few months we left, and eventually the group dissolved.

We once again found ourselves alone.

Not a Jew, yet not a Christian. It's a lonely place to be. There is no real home for us, no community, neither religiously nor socially. We have two daughters whom we homeschool and have yet to find a social group to which we can belong. Most of the homeschool groups here in East Texas are Christian-based and require agreeing to their statement of faith before joining. If a group is not Christian, then they are often very worldly and not the caliber of friends we seek for our daughters. My heart aches to find our place. I have cried out to Hashem for answers and for help, but He, in His infinite wisdom, is still writing this part of our story.

One difference I have noticed between Christians and Jews when faced with a problem is that Christians will pray and sit back and wait on God to act, but Jews will pray and then get busy working towards a solution, allowing God to guide them in their efforts. This is something I need to work on in finding community for our family; to actively work at it and not just sit back expecting God to provide the solution.

We have considered converting, and may at some point. But if we convert and want community, we will have to move again. The last thing I want is to upheave my family's life once more. Especially since we only have a few short years left with our oldest until she graduates. We also have our extended family to consider and the effect it would have on them if we converted.

In the Christian faith, as I'm sure you are aware, you must "accept Jesus as your Lord and Savior," and in the Baptist denomination, follow that up with baptism in your church. Our oldest daughter did all this when we were still in church, but our younger daughter did not. So now both sets of grandparents are really concerned that she has not "made her decision for Christ" because, for them, that means if she dies, she's going to hell, which is very scary for any Christian grandparent to think about. It is very real for them and they view it as the single most important decision in your entire life.

Since my parents no longer discuss Biblical matters with us, they have only mentioned it a few times, but I know as my youngest daughter gets older, it will become a more pressing matter for them. It also puts me in an awkward position when they want to have our daughters spend some time with them over the summer because if they stay with them on a Sunday or Wednesday, they'll take them to church, and I know without us there they will talk to them about Jesus in hopes of getting my youngest to accept him.

But it's hard to say no and not let them go because these are their only two grandchildren. Besides that, I dread them finding out that I no longer believe in Jesus. It would crush them. It would be more devastating for them to find out I have denounced Jesus than for me to die.

I realize this sounds overly dramatic, but for them to think that they will not see me in heaven after they die would be more than they can bear. How can I bring that kind of devastation upon them? I already struggle with guilt every time we're not at their table for Christmas or Easter, and I know they are at home alone, not able to celebrate with their grandchildren because I know the emotional pain it causes them. I struggle a lot with honoring my parents but not compromising my beliefs. There's no instruction manual. Nothing tells us step by step how to walk out of the Christian faith without hurting your Christian family members.

We have also considered the idea of converting and not telling our family. However, it would still cause problems because our conversion would severely limit our ability to eat with them, or go out to traditional restaurants with them. They would obviously ask why and we would be forced to tell them about our conversion.

Something I feel strongly about is the need to be prepared to care for my parents as they age. As an only child, their care falls squarely in my lap, as it should. If I convert now, I feel it will not only put a further wedge between us and our family, that is already in a delicate relationship. It will also impede my ability to care for them adequately when the time comes. These are the things I am praying about and weighing as I consider what the right path for our family is at this time.

For now, we are Noahides who choose to observe more of the Torah than is required out of our love and devotion to Hashem.

Because sharing with people that you no longer believe Jesus is messiah can be tricky when it comes to friendships, we have only shared with one family friend, and only because they point blank asked us. We had told them that we had been attending the shul and they wanted to know what our current beliefs about Jesus and messiah were, and how that played out while attending a Conservative synagogue. I was able to explain our journey in learning more about who Jesus really was (and who he wasn't) and the steps in our understanding that led us to where we are today. While our friends don't agree with our conclusions, it was a huge relief to find that they would not drop our friendship because we no longer believe in Jesus in the same way.

It would be nice if all conversations with friends and family would go this way. It's hard to remain silent and not share your new beliefs. But at times, it feels like walking a tightrope between not sharing anything for the sake of maintaining relationships or sharing it all and potentially going through the heartbreak of losing those relationships.

Lately, there have been a few Jewish families from the original group that left the local shul who have begun meeting again in each other's homes for Shabbat and we have joined them. It is not large, and there are no children our daughters' ages, but I am thankful for them. It does our souls good to be close to the Jewish people and to continue to learn from them.

This journey is not easy, and the path is definitely not straight. There are many ups and downs, doubts and revelations, joys and frustrations. Through it all, I see Hashem testing my emunah[71]. Will I trust Him and be faithful even when it feels lonely and I don't know where I'm headed?

It is difficult to wrap up my story with a nice and tidy ending, because truly we haven't reached the end of our journey. We are still very much on the path and uncertain of where it will ultimately lead. Will we eventually convert? Will we one day move to Israel? Will we remain Noahides and somehow assist others on their journey? I may not know, but I know the One who does. So while we may

---

[71] faith

not be completely alone among the nations, we are definitely lonely among the nations.

But even though, at times, our path looks bleak and lonesome, we are never truly alone. Hashem is with us every step of the way, and in that, I can take comfort.

> *Ginni Gamble married her high-school sweetheart 21 years ago. They now reside in East Texas with their two beautiful teenage daughters and two fluffy cats, Nacho and Whiskers. Formerly an assistant buyer for JCPenney, she left the corporate world to raise and homeschool her family. She thrives on coffee, meaningful conversation and studying Torah. Ginni can be reached at ginnigamble@mac.com.*

What Exactly Did Jesus Die For?

Teresa Hutslar

I can't remember a time when God wasn't an important part of my life. Although my parents weren't particularly religious themselves, my grandmother saw to it that I was christened in the Catholic church and attended Mass with her. By the time I was in elementary school, my parents were separated and my mother found God and community in an evangelical Christian church.

My sisters and I would all attend that church with her on Sundays, but I would still attend Mass with my grandmother on Saturdays. This back-and-forth continued even after my parents reconciled and we moved to a different state. My mother insisted on me attending church with her on Sundays, but my father insisted I attend Mass with the neighbors on Saturdays because he wanted me to continue to learn the Catholic faith.

By my preteen years, I struggled with much of the Catholic doctrine. I had questions that nobody could or would answer. Some of my main questions were about praying to, and the worship of Mary, whom I was sure was a righteous woman, but we shouldn't worship her. I had questions about the Trinity, but I was told it was a mystery that we couldn't understand. I also questioned the Eucharist, to the point of refusing to take it anymore much to my grandmother's horror. I just couldn't bring myself to literally eat the body and drink the blood of Jesus. It felt so wrong.

After asking someone at the Catholic church about my concerns, I was told I shouldn't be reading my Bible on my own. I didn't like that answer, so I decided to ask one of the pastors at my mother's church the same questions. His answers didn't give me the satisfaction I was hoping for. He just went on a rant about how the Catholic church had perverted the teachings of Jesus.

At this point, my parents decided that I would stop attending Mass and attend church with my mother. With my new rebellious streak and my unending, questioning curiosity, my parents felt that maybe attending both churches was causing some confusion in me.

The next year, church became routine as I started losing interest in religion and gaining more interest in becoming a teen and having fun. One day, my mother found an invitation to a church youth group among my school things. Earlier that day at school, two students were handing invitations out, so I quickly shoved it in my backpack and forgot about it. She told me years later that she would go through my backpack every day and that's how she found it. Not liking the path I was heading down, she announced that she was taking me to the very next meeting.

This youth group was nothing like I had ever seen in a church. It was large, with hundreds of students attending. Missing from the room were the large crosses and stained glass I was used to. Instead, it had a stage with a band playing rock-style worship music, a light show, a teaching geared towards teen issues like drinking and drugs, and very often, a skit with a message. It was usually about someone who refused Jesus and then died, waking up in hell. The skit was followed by an altar call to accept Jesus into your heart.

Although I was completely overwhelmed at first, I ended up enjoying it after some time. The whole atmosphere appealed to me as a teen girl, plus I met great friends there that I am still friends with today. It's even where I met my husband.

Week after week, we heard messages on the topic of spending eternity in hell and on how, because of Adam and Eve eating the apple, sin came into the world and cursed humanity. Every week, I would respond to that altar call and "get saved" to make sure I didn't go to hell. The pastor noticed that, sat me down and explained there was no need to respond every time I visited, to which I replied, "But you don't know what I've done all week!"

While we were sitting, I took the opportunity to ask him my questions I had for years and the new ones I had on original sin and eternal hellfire. As much as I tried, I couldn't reconcile those things in my heart. He told me these were the core tenets of the Christian faith, and we can't question God on them. God is just and righteous and we humans are not. That's why we see an eternal hellfire as harsh, and he sees it as just. He ended with, "You just have to have faith, Teresa." I was devastated since I highly respected him and thought he would have all the answers.

After realizing that I was not going to get the answers I wanted, I decided I needed to focus more on faith and less on questioning. I just needed to believe, right?

Little did I know, this was my first lesson in emunah[72]. In fact, if I could summarize my entire journey in just one word it would be Emunah. I've learned that faith, or emunah, goes way beyond belief. It endures even in the face of questions. It is a trust in God that He is in control of everything in our lives, even down to the most minute detail. Emunah is a trust, that as it grows, causes your whole life to change.

As I married and began having children, the small lessons in faith kept coming. We felt that as parents, the best thing we could

---

[72] faith

teach our children was to trust God. We taught them a faith that would carry with them no matter where they went in life or what questions they had, a faith that would endure even when life was hard…especially when life was hard.

We even came up with a family motto that they all still remember to this day. Our motto was, *"We are a family set apart by God for a purpose. We live and walk by faith while being a light to the world."*

As I taught my children about faith, I still had the questions I stopped asking out loud in the back of my mind, pulling at me, begging to be answered. So many times during the years, I had seen God's faithfulness in my life. I was blessed beyond anything I could have imagined. I was married to a wonderful man and had eight beautiful children. I had an amazing career as a nurse, even though I decided to pause that for a few years to homeschool my children.

With all that I had lived and experienced in my life, why wasn't I content? Why couldn't I just believe and leave it at that?

I knew He heard my prayers and answered them over and over. I had seen literal miracles in my life. I often joked that I had a pipeline straight to God. So why didn't the questions leave me at night when it was quiet and dark? Was I broken? Who was I to question God? Why didn't anyone else I know have questions? How come my family could all just accept what they were taught and never question it?

I realized I was having a crisis of faith, so I needed to get some answers. After talking to my husband, we decided to investigate a different denomination outside of the Assembly of God church we were attending. We started attending a small fundamentalist Baptist church for about two years, but ended up right back where we came from. While I appreciated their love for memorizing scripture verses, it just didn't feel like home. I look back at that time and I can see now that this was the beginning of separation, when we were beginning to realize that we weren't fitting in with the church anymore.

I then dove into studying reformed theology. What I found there was appalling to me. Their doctrine of total depravity was depressing, and the belief in predestination reeked with pride. I read about Martin Luther and his disgusting antisemitic beliefs and realized I couldn't align myself with any movement associated with him.

At the time, it didn't really hit me that the whole Protestant movement was started by a raging antisemite with his words still inspiring violence against the Jewish people even today.

While I was studying these things out, my husband and I had enrolled in classes to become licensed ministers. I was teaching a women's Bible study at our church. I was hoping that a deep dive into my religion taught by those who know better than me would settle things. Additionally, we just wanted to serve our community.

We ended up quitting those classes with only two classes left because our beliefs were slowly changing. We knew we couldn't in good conscience represent them as a denomination. I will say that taking those classes caused me to start seeking answers outside of Christianity completely.

After a class on world religions, I had a random thought, "Why don't I see what Judaism's concept of hell is?"

Even though I was raised in the Catholic and Assembly of God's churches, I was also raised with a deep love of Israel and the Jewish people. My grandmother is Polish and told me stories about her family. They had lost their land, and because of that, some of her mother's family immigrated to America. Those who stayed fled elsewhere, and some even died in the Holocaust. She didn't know more than bits and pieces about that side of the family since her mother died young and didn't talk much about her life before America.

That gave me a very deep soul connection that I couldn't explain as a child, one that has only grown as an adult, but my first real love of Israel came from my evangelical Christian mama. She always taught me that Israel and the Jewish people were the apple of God's eye. His beloved children. I remember her praying fervently for protection and peace in Israel. To this day, she has a shofar and prayer shawl she keeps on display.

As I studied out the Jewish concept of hell and original sin, I realized I couldn't find them in ancient Jewish thought. So, where did these concepts come from? As I dove deeper into the study of hell, I could feel my heart hardening to the faith I had practiced for so long. Why were we taught that we had free will to serve God but were also taught that we would burn for all eternity if we didn't accept Jesus? Not just for a few years or even a lifetime but for a never-ending eternity. Did we really have free will at that point?

It was at that point I began to fervently pray every day, "God, give me a heart of flesh instead of a heart of stone. I just want to know the truth." I knew that God had never left me, and He wouldn't now. I didn't want to lose my faith completely.

Looking back, I can see that this was my next big lesson in emunah.

I can't tell you why, but at this point I felt a strong compulsion to teach the children the Jewish feasts as part of our homeschooling. I also felt I should stop eating pork. How and why I had these thoughts in the middle of a crisis, I have no clue, except God. It was then that our whole family dove into the beginnings of learning the Torah while thinking we must be the only people doing this. As we learned more, we slowly started working our way out of leadership with the church and eventually left the church altogether. It was a natural separation that happened. It just wasn't home there anymore.

Knowing the importance of community, my husband and I knew we had to find something for our family. We connected with an amazing fellowship for the next few years where we were able to just rest and reset our brains. The time came though when we knew we needed to make a physical move to a different state. My husband's business was dwindling, and we desired a larger community for our children. We ended up connecting with a Hebrew Roots group in the state we wanted to move to. It felt like it would be a safe place for us to be with like-minded friends for us and our children.

Things were good for a while, but we slowly saw a change. We noticed more people becoming afraid of "traditions" and leery of the Jewish calendar. They began to have doubts about when the Sabbath started. Instead of people asking questions and thinking our Sabbath traditions were interesting, we were nicknamed the "local Talmudists." We were also warned multiple times not to jump into the ditch of Judaism.

When we first started looking into the truths of Torah years back, we felt that we should learn from the ones the Torah had been given to and had practiced it for thousands of years. Where better to learn from than the Jewish people themselves? We didn't see it as a ditch. We saw it as a privilege.

The more we learned and the more commandments we took on, just like the Jewish people do all over the world, the more order came into our lives. The more order and shalom[73] we had in our home, the more chaotic the Hebrew Roots movement and even the church looked.

I couldn't understand the fear people had when it felt like just one drop of Torah truth we learned from the rabbis gave a depth of learning that we had never experienced before. It gave us the spiritual food we had craved for so long.

It became glaringly apparent that replacement theology had taken root here. Even with us now being the odd man out with our local friends, we all still tried to get along and focus on common

---

[73] peace

beliefs instead of differences. This was okay, until we decided to add another level of commitment.

We already knew that following the commandments brought order and shalom, but we learned they also bring separation. Each time we took on a new level of observance, it separated us from the rest of the world. We realize now that this is exactly what they're supposed to do.

We accepted the separation from the church in the beginning; we even handled it gracefully with our extended family as they adjusted to our new way of life, but with our spiritual family? This was so much harder for us.

We felt our circle shrinking even more. As the social events lessened, it gave me the time I needed to really dive in and study. I am so grateful for that time. I feel like it was a gift from God. As I dove into learning Torah and what Judaism teaches, I was finally getting the answers to questions I had had for so long. I felt like I finally had the pieces of the puzzle I had been missing since I was a girl.

Instead of believing that I was born sinful and there was nothing I could do to earn forgiveness, I was praying, "My God, the soul you placed within me is pure. You created it, you formed it, you breathed it into me…"

I read the verses in Micah 7, "Who is a God like you, who pardons iniquity and forgives transgression for the remnant of his heritage? He does not maintain his wrath forever for He desires to do kindness. He will again show us mercy, He will suppress our iniquities, and you will cast all of their sins into the depths of the sea."

I read in Lamentations 3, "The kindness of the Lord has not ended, His mercies are not spent. They are renewed every morning. Ample is your Grace!"

The more I saw forgiveness and mercy in the Tanach[74], the more I saw that anyone could make teshuvah[75]. A question I dared not ask needed to be answered at this point. If there was already forgiveness and a path to draw close to God for those who repented in Tanach, what exactly did Jesus die for?

This was a question I never expected to ask and certainly didn't go looking for. It found me. It's one I answered slowly and with great trepidation. I even took a few breaks from it so I wouldn't unravel all my beliefs. I knew in my heart what the answer was. I think I always knew what the answer was, but I was afraid. I was afraid I would deconstruct too far and be left with nothing. God was so faithful and I didn't want to turn my back on Him. I also didn't want to be wrong when the stakes were so high.

It finally hit me that so much of what I had given Jesus credit for was God all along. The one true God was with me all those years. He's the one who heard my prayers and He's the one who answered me. The miracles I saw, He did. I was still a daughter of the Most High King.

I remembered the verses in Isaiah 12 that we pray every week. "Behold, God is my salvation. I will trust and will not be afraid; for the Lord God is my strength and my song, and He has become my salvation. Therefore, with joy you shall draw water out of the wells of salvation."

I began to see a beautiful story of redemption for humanity, one born out of love with a God who is so merciful. That's when I had peace in my heart. I would not fear, but I would trust with joy. God was my salvation!

Just as Lamentations says, "The Lord is my portion, I say with a

---

[74] Hebrew bible

[75] repent

full heart; Therefore, I will hope in Him. The Lord is good to those who trust in Him, To the one who seeks him."

I don't have time to talk about all my thoughts and feelings on Jesus here, but I truly believe that each step in my journey was necessary for where I am today. I just pray and thank God that He has given me wisdom to see truth, something I have prayed for, for years.

The more I learned the more alive spiritually, emotionally, intellectually and even physically I felt. I wanted to share it with the world, but I also wanted to keep it to myself because I was very aware that our beliefs were becoming very different and even incompatible with Christianity and the messianic movement.

We decided to keep quiet and learn more as a family. Our children needed that time. They were on this journey with us and just as invested. We needed time to tell our extended family what was going on. We also had a child working in Israel with a Christian organization, so we wanted to consider him. Lastly, it allowed us time to continue attending our fellowship for our children's community. Whether that was right or wrong, I cannot say.

That is until October 7. I can't explain what happened very well at all, but a huge chasm opened. An invisible line was drawn, and you either stood with Israel and the Jewish people or you didn't. We quickly realized we were on the side not many were on. This was what finally separated us completely from the fellowship we attended.

At that point, we truly no longer "belonged" anywhere - not in the church, not in the messianic movement, not in Judaism. This separation has left us without a larger spiritual community and a handful of friends.

Speaking of friends, can I stop and say how thankful I am that we do have friends that are walking this same path, at the same time alongside us? It has been a lifeline at times, even if we are in different states. I can't even imagine not having them by our side.

That still doesn't change the fact that my children are lonely. If it was just my husband and me, it would be different, but what about them? This is the time in their lives where a vibrant spiritual community is so important. The loneliness I see in them at times is almost unbearable for my mama heart to watch.

For me, I'm married and have my family. For them? Not being Christian and not being Jewish leaves them in a no man's land. I cannot even describe the guilt I feel at times. I will also say that I am so proud of the strength and resolve they have shown. They have defended their faith fiercely; they have encouraged us to keep going and hold us accountable when we need it.

I know we are in a very small circle of not belonging anywhere, but our emunah has not wavered. We pray daily as a family that Hashem will guide us on our next step towards home. Until then, we have started classes online with a rabbi who is a conversion mentor.

Our story isn't finished yet, so I don't know exactly where we will end up. All I know is that God has always been faithful in my life, and I trust Him.

Teresa has been married to the love of her life, Scott, for 32 years. They have been blessed with eight children, and eight grandchildren with more coming. She worked as a NICU nurse for years before putting her career aside to homeschool her children. She has a passion for sharing the joy of a life centered around the home and having a large family. She also uses her medical background to show others how to heal the body using natural medicine. In what spare time she has, usually late at night, she loves to read, study and research Biblical topics. You can reach her at alifeathome@gmail.com

Shifting Belief: Embracing Faith in the God of Jesus Alone

Paushali Lass

I was raised in a non-religious household in India, where the belief in God and the importance of being morally right were emphasized, but there was no specific religion that my family followed. During my university years in the UK, I came to faith in Jesus and became a Christian. However, it was the fact that Jesus was a Jew that truly made me feel connected with him. For some reason, from a very young age, I remember having a deep curiosity about the Jewish people.

As I grew in my faith, I developed a love for reading the Scriptures. In both my difficult and joyous moments, it was the Psalms that kept me going. I also looked at Jesus, my saviour, as someone who was always with me through the thick and the thin. Jesus was in the Psalms and Jesus was the one who revealed the Scripture to me. He was like the one who God used to speak to my life.

With an academic and research background, I generally love to dig deep and investigate texts. This ingrained characteristic led me to the habit of also delving deep into Scripture on various topics. However, the more I read the New Testament through the years, the more confused I became regarding several topics. I found it hard to define a few things that the Bible talked about and started discovering discrepancies between "Old Testament" and New Testament interpretations. Here are a few examples:

What exactly is the "Good News" that the Gospels keep referring to? How do I explain the Trinity and reconcile it with the concept of "One God" as I read in Deuteronomy 6:4?

I had more questions than answers when I read Paul's letters. Even though I was told we are no longer required to keep the Law, why is it that Jesus said he did not come to abolish the Law, but to fulfil it? What does "to fulfil it" even mean? Furthermore, God said in the "Old Testament" of the Christian Bible that His commandments were forever.

I kept wondering about the fate of good people like my late dear gran who had never heard about Jesus - why should they be condemned to eternal separation simply because they never knew him?

In my pursuit of understanding the "Old Testament" better, I began studying Hebrew and bought the JPS[76] Tanakh 18 years ago, hoping to better grasp the Jewish perspective and how they interpret the Scriptures. My goal all those years ago was to prove to the Jewish people that Jesus was the Messiah. Little did I know, however, that Jews do not interpret verses in the same way Christians do. Years later I learnt (it is an ongoing learning process) that many Hebrew Bible verses have been significantly adjusted to fit the Christian narrative (I'll explore this further later).

Over time, I became busy raising children and was deeply involved in church life, leading Bible studies for women and immersing myself in Scripture. While I don't recall pastors teaching about biblical prophecies concerning Israel in the churches my husband

---

[76] Jewish Publication Society

and I attended in different countries we had the privilege of living in, I always knew the Jews were God's chosen people and that His promises to Israel are everlasting. It was clear to me that if you love the God of the Bible, you must love Israel. Strangely, I even had a desire to die in the land of Israel. Though I loved Israel, my understanding of biblical prophecy about it has only deepened in the past seven years.

Continuing regular Bible studies, about eight years ago, I really felt like Hashem[77] is leading me more and more into studying the topics of exile, the ten lost tribes as well as the end time prophecies. Gradually, I started seeing how everything was centered around Israel and verses which I had previously learnt about in churches as applicable to us personally[78] were in fact about Israel/Judah. Another thing I realized as I dug into the Tanakh is that while Hashem's message is consistent about the *end of days*, the message concerning the same is not consistent or easily understood in the New Testament. For example, the more I read the Book of Revelation and tried to match it with Matthew 24 or 1 and 2 Thessalonians, the more perplexed I became.

Then came the pivotal realization: As Christians, we often grow up learning Scripture out of context. Much of the church teaching touches on verses from the Tanakh without providing the background information. This leads to "Old Testament" passages being applied to us personally, even when they were originally meant for Israel. This realization pushed me toward a deeper search for truth.

---

[77] Literally, Hebrew for "the Name" and used to refer to God

[78] e.g. "I know the plans I have for you", declares the Lord, "plans to prosper you and not to harm you - Jeremiah 29:11

Hashem's Guidance

I am forever grateful for the first time I was in Israel. Through Hashem's providence, I came into contact with some wonderful Orthodox Jews there, from whom I could learn so much. Since my first visit to Israel, I have developed contact with several pro-Israel Christian ministries in Germany (where I live) and have tried to build bridges between Jewish and Christian communities and bring Christian groups to Israel to connect with the Jewish world. One of the things that always made me uncomfortable in this context was the Christian focus on evangelizing Jews. I must say I have also met several wonderful Christians, especially from Germany, who unconditionally love the Jewish people, no strings attached. However, this is still only a minority group. Unlike many other Christians who visit Israel, Hashem seemed to lead me toward Jews, not Christians or Messianic believers[79] living in the Land.

As I got to know more and more Orthodox Jews, a crucial question kept coming to my mind: How is it that Orthodox Jews—who live so close to God and are part of His chosen nation—are doomed to hell if they don't accept Jesus? I searched Scripture thoroughly and found no reference suggesting this. I also began to feel a deep sympathy for secular Jews. I wondered why, despite their heritage and connection to the God of Israel, they seemed to be seeking spiritual fulfillment elsewhere - whether in India, in other faiths, or even in Jesus.

A Journey of Learning

I started studying the Torah, and with each passing day, my understanding deepened. I was humbled by how much Torah-observant

---

[79] Jews who believe in Jesus

Jews knew, and I recognized how arrogant I had been in thinking they needed help from Jesus or the New Testament. That realization was eye-opening.

Evangelism had never sat comfortably with me. I could share my personal story with others, as to how I came to faith in Jesus, but I felt uncomfortable trying to convince someone else to believe in Jesus.

During my earlier attempts to prove to a Jewish friend that Jesus was the Messiah, I came across resources from Rabbi Tovia Singer - an incredibly knowledgeable man, almost like a walking and talking Bible! Now that I have learned some Hebrew and continue to study, I see more clearly the inconsistencies, phantom verses, and contradictions in the New Testament, as Rabbi Singer often points out. However, I must mention here that to me, Jesus is not a mere nobody like he is probably for most Jewish people. After all, I learnt about the God of Abraham, Isaac and Jacob through the person of Jesus as I believed him to be.

However, as I dive deeper into my journey, the more I uncover, the more I'm left with feelings of confusion and contradiction. The inconsistencies are impossible to ignore now. Learning Hebrew has opened my eyes to things I never saw before, like how Scriptures such as Psalm 110:1 and Isaiah 9:6 have been mistranslated or mis-interpreted by Christians to view Jesus as the Messiah. As I study the Tanakh from an unadulterated version, I can't help but notice not only the differences between the Christian interpretation and the original intended meaning, but I am also beginning to understand the layers of meaning that I never fully grasped in the Christian context. It's like a veil is being lifted, revealing truths that had been obscured for so long.

For years, I was taught one thing, and now, in reading the Scriptures through a Jewish lens, it's as if the ground beneath me is shifting. I've spent so many years internalizing Christian teachings - understanding the Messiah in one way, only to realize that this doesn't align with the Jewish understanding of who the Messiah is. It's not someone to be worshipped. It's a figure who leads people toward God, not toward himself.

That realization leaves me grappling with the question: why was I lied to all these years? I don't blame my teachers—they didn't know any better, but **the church not only cut itself off from its roots, it deliberately changed the Hebrew Scripture on occasions more than once**! The Hebrew Scriptures were suddenly relegated to the status of "Old Testament," as if they were something separate, obsolete or less important, when in reality, they hold the key to understanding the full picture.

I must give a concrete example here as to how Christian Bibles have altered the Hebrew Scriptures to fit the Christian narrative.

In Luke 4:16-18, on the Shabbat day, Jesus reads from the Torah scroll verses from Isaiah 61:1-2. If he read from the Torah scroll, then the original Hebrew Masoretic text would have been read. In this original Hebrew text though, there is no mention of "recovery of sight for the blind." Did the New Testament deliberately add this to fit the action of Jesus healing the blind? Or where did this come from and why did it suddenly get included? On close reading of the New Testament, I find many of the cross-references to the original Scriptures from the Tanakh are somehow adjusted, either text added in or some text taken away! This really made my alarm bells go off and I was left with many troubling questions about the faith that I held so dear.

Moreover, when I think about my Jewish friends, especially those who are Torah observant and live in awe of God, I can't grasp why they would be condemned because they don't believe in Jesus as their Messiah. They live in reverence, in fear of God, and yet I've been taught that they're somehow outside of salvation. This dissonance is something I can't reconcile.

As I mentioned, I always felt uncomfortable with evangelism; it never sat right with me. At the same time for my own life, I felt like I wasn't doing enough for God if I didn't "share the gospel," but at the same time, I knew that God loves me as I am. He wants me to draw closer to Him, to live in a way that reflects His values—Micah 6:8 tells me that's what He asks: to do justice, love mercy, and walk humbly with Him. As I was delving deeper into my spiritual journey, a very important moment in modern history struck the whole world and it literally turned everything upside down!

That important moment was the October 7th massacre in Israel committed by Hamas and the Islamic Jihadists. The indifference of much of the church in the face of such tragedy confirmed everything I had been wrestling with. I saw just how separate our identities had become. I saw clearly at that moment how the church values align very differently with what I read in the Bible. I of course do not want to generalise here as there are millions of Christians who absolutely stand with Israel. They are the ones who read both "Old and New Testaments" of their Christian Bibles and know the place of the Jewish people in God's eyes. However, a large majority of the church has been largely silent. They go on with their ministries and programs as if the world is going on as normal.

The church wants to evangelize, to bring people to Jesus. But that's not my path anymore. I am not going to try and change people's minds. God is sovereign and He will guide the truth seekers in the path that He has for every individual. My heart's desire is that people, Jews and Gentiles alike, do *Tshuva*[80] - to return to God, to reconnect, to repent. That feels like the most authentic and meaningful way forward.

---

[80] Literally, Hebrew for return and used to mean repentance, also spelled teshuva

Conclusion

Ultimately, in my mind, this is what I have come to realize: Jesus is not the Messiah - at least, not in the way the Scriptures describe a Jewish Messiah. In a recent study of the Parashah from Ki Tisa, which focuses on the golden calf and the golden dust (Exodus 32), my teacher shared an important lesson: God can easily and swiftly tear down idols. This felt remarkably similar to what had happened to me. To my surprise, I found myself quickly and easily detached from the idea of Jesus as my redeemer. In the end, I realized that my faith had always been in Hashem.

I don't judge others for their beliefs. They are free to believe as they wish. But for me, I cannot, with integrity, call the New Testament "Scripture," given its inconsistencies with the Tanakh and the way it has corrupted the Hebrew Scriptures to fit the Christian narrative. Over time, it has evolved into a Roman religion.

The question remains though: who is Jesus? For me, he is a savior in the sense that he led me to the knowledge of Hashem, the One True God of Israel. Even if I were to set aside everything in the New Testament, his teachings emphasize that we are to do what the Torah teachers tell us, and that the law will never be abolished.

Through Christianity, I came to faith in the one true God of Israel. I now place my faith in the God of Jesus alone, not in Jesus himself. I firmly believe that there is, and must not be, any other God besides Hashem. He is not a man (Numbers 23, Psalm 146), and He will never change His mind.

I love the people who I have actively engaged with in my Christian life, the people who I have laughed with, prayed with and had wonderful fellowship with. While my love for them does not change, I do admit I feel increasingly uncomfortable in certain situations with the very same people. The moments which make me feel most that way are when we communicate with God through prayer. I find it particularly hard to hear when people pray *to* Jesus, rather than to God.

As part of my ongoing journey, I'd like to address a key point for helping truth-seeking Christians: many have raised the valid concern that not everyone speaks or can learn Hebrew. I invite a discussion on how scholars and former Christians can collaborate to find meaningful solutions for those without Hebrew knowledge. It would be valuable to see more accessible educational resources that help Christians understand the Tanakh in context and identify discrepancies between the "Old and New Testaments."

In my journey of constant discovery of what the Tanakh actually says as opposed to what I was taught to understand and regurgitate, I do want to highlight the support of my husband in this deep soulful enquiry. He doesn't walk the same path I do (yet), but he listens, he understands. That means more to me than I can put into words. But I still feel so alone. I know that if I were to fully express my beliefs to most people, I'd be seen as someone who has lost their salvation, someone doomed to destruction. And that fear is real—feeling like I'm being rejected by the very people who once felt like my spiritual family. It feels uncomfortable these days to be around people who discuss Jesus as God or refer to New Testament verses as life's answers, as I no longer align with those beliefs.

I often find myself in a state of limbo, neither fully here nor there. What do I mean by that? I am much more closely aligned with the Jewish people who take their Judaism seriously than with Christians who love Israel. I fight day and night in the social media space as well as in real life for Israel and combating antisemitism as if I were Jewish. But I am "officially" not. I do feel like I have a Jewish neshama, a Jewish soul and while I am not Jewish, I am drawn to the teachings and principles laid out in the Tanakh and aspire to live by them. My perspective goes beyond merely identifying as a Noahide[81] and this is the current state I am in.

The loneliness is compounded by the fact that I live in a European country, where I feel caught between two worlds. I'm neither here nor there. I don't feel fully at home in the culture, and I can't fully connect with the way people practice religion here. But when I go to Israel, everything changes. There, I feel a sense of community - a connection to something greater, something deeply rooted in history and faith. It's a place where I can be with people who understand what it means to live in alignment with their beliefs, and that's something I don't find where I am now.

This journey is certainly not easy, and sometimes it feels like I'm losing everything. But deep down, I know that I am seeking truth. I'm not turning away from God; Far from it. I'm just seeking a deeper, more authentic relationship with Him.

Paushali Lass is a writer, researcher, and educator, based in Germany and originally from India. She has also lived in the UK and Singapore. She advocates for Israel and educates communities about its truth, as well as brings groups to Israel to connect with its people. Paushali lives with her husband and five children in Germany. You can reach her at paushali14@ gmail.com.

---

[81] A Noahide refers to a person who follows the Seven Laws of Noah, which are considered universal moral principles in Jewish tradition and apply to all of humanity.

The Silent Struggle

Shannon Nuszen

In silence, I wrestle, alone in the night,
A crisis of faith—no hope, no light.[82]
This isn't just belief; it's my very life,
My core, my heart, my identity's strife.

The texts are clear, their truth laid bare,
But to voice it aloud—how could I dare?
Who would believe me, who could I tell,
That my faith now feels like a fragile shell?

I've never known such despair, such fear,
But Jesus is with me—wait, are you here?[83]
Were you ever there, this voice in my mind?
Who have I prayed to, and trusted in kind?

It's too much to bear, this weight, this doubt,
That presence within I can't live without.
I'm scared to speak, to let anyone see,
Yet the facts before me demand honesty.

Alone in this battle, afraid yet awake,
I stand on the edge of the truths I must take.
For though I am trembling, lost in the fray,
The search for what's real won't let me stay.[84]

---

[82] Psalm 22:1-2
[83] Lamentations 3:40-41
[84] Psalm 42:5-6

Shannon Nuszen, a former Evangelical Christian missionary, was raised in the world of Christian scriptural polemics as the daughter of a minister. Once deeply involved in the Christian messianic movement, she later converted to Judaism and has since dedicated her life to exposing missionary tactics targeting Jews. Drawing from her firsthand experience, she educates Jewish communities worldwide on the dangers of deceptive proselytization. Shannon is the founder of Beyneynu, an organization that monitors missionary activity worldwide and advocates for proper boundaries and guidelines with faith-based organizations. You can reach her at Shannon@beyneynu.com.

From Dirty Sinner to Proud Noahide

Vanessa Ramsey

Transport yourself back to the 1970s. Imagine a little 8-year-old girl playing with her little brother and dolls. She is wearing a long white robe and standing in front of the fireplace. She has set up candles, cups and other accouterments, pretending to be a priest going through a communion ceremony. She shushes her little brother and continues on through her play-acting.

Yes, this was me. Strange as the scene may seem, I see the soul of a little girl who desired to be close to her Creator with the purity and sincerity of a child.

Both sides of my family were Roman Catholic. I always loved church: the structure of the service, the liturgy, beautiful buildings with stained glass windows, holy water and the community. The opposite side of this lovely picture of Catholicism was the brutal imagery of crucifixion, Jesus' betrayal and the 12 stations of the cross, which were imprinted into my subconscious.

Shortly after this point, my searching mother, followed by my father, got "saved" and promptly left the Catholic Church. With a newfound gospel message, my extended family was told that if they didn't accept Jesus, they were going to hell. This situation resulted in burnt bridges with these family members. I carried a sadness and great loss to no longer have relationships with my cousins, aunts and uncles due to my parents' beliefs and actions.

My family ran the gamut of Protestant Evangelical churches. With this change came a clear break from the ethos of Catholicism and a move into a foreign world of old-time gospel hymns and pulpit-pounding pastors who delivered regular, terrifying sermons about how Jesus died for my sins to save me from eternal hellfire and damnation.

A change in what I was taught came with my parents' newfound beliefs. It was no longer about getting to heaven with good deeds, specific behaviors and prayers. Now, I was told that to get to heaven, I had to "accept Jesus into your heart as your lord and savior."

I remember the night I was "saved" and baptized at the Baptist Church, solely because I was terrified by the latest sermon about burning in hell and how the return of Jesus would leave me behind and all alone. Fear and loathing. I was afraid of going to hell if I didn't take the golden "Jesus" ticket and feelings of guilt and shame because my sins caused Jesus to suffer. This laid a foundation of self-hatred for the next few decades.

In Sunday school, with lessons and songs, I was taught that Jesus was my friend and he saved me from the wrath of God. I grew up thinking I was a dirty sinner who could never truly be good, which is why I had to accept Jesus because he "paid it all." Jesus was supposed to make me free with his sacrifice for my sins, but I felt anything but free.

Eventually, my parents found their place in a Christian cult. This group followed the teachings of J.N. Darby.[85] They were in a very

---

[85] https://en.wikipedia.org/wiki/John_Nelson_Darby

insular bubble and contact with the rest of the world was frowned upon. I was pulled out of school and homeschooled. I was told I needed to wear skirts and that I must cover my head when reading the Bible or praying.

The thoughts and opinions of women, much less a young girl, were not valued. I felt dismissed and ignored. Higher education was unacceptable because we were not supposed to mingle with the world. This indoctrination continued from age nine throughout my teens and into my early 20s. The cult became my only community and it was not easy to disentangle from it.

As I moved into my 20s, several things occurred that precipitated much change in my life. I had married young to get out of my house and then subsequently divorced, and eventually, my own parents divorced. My life was in disarray for a time. But with these painful experiences came new opportunities.

I enrolled at a local university and worked at a local bookstore. I made new friends and I saw there was more to life beyond the cult. This pushed on my pre-existing boundaries and self-limiting beliefs and I felt open to exploring my relationship with God. I left the cult.

As some prescience to my future, I registered for a university class in Israel in 2000, but it was canceled due to the Second Intifada. I studied to obtain a science major and explored the theory of evolution. This never made sense to me because it could never explain human consciousness. At the bookstore, I read a wide range of spiritual books.

Through this exploration, I wasn't attending any church, yet I continued to learn and grow spiritually. I read the Bible, prayed and navigated life. This practice kept me tethered to God, yet I still felt like something was missing. I wanted to know the realness of God! I desired a deeper connection with my Creator and wanted God to be in my daily life in a real way, not just someone in Whom I believed.

I had this picture in my consciousness of looking over and around something (or someone) to try to find Him.

Eventually, I remarried to a good, God-fearing man. As we moved through life together we wanted a closer connection to God and guidance with our young family. All we knew was to attend a church. We lived in a town where you could throw a rock and hit the next church building down the road. How to know where to go? We knew we didn't want to join one of the mega-churches. We wanted a more intimate connection, a place where we were known and understood. So we found a local church and began attending.

Concurrently my husband and I were taking online classes with Koinonia Institute, a Christian school meant for deeper learning of the Bible. My heart was so happy digging into the meaning of words in Scripture in their original language! While some of the learning was familiar and confirmed my past Christian instruction, it also expanded my thinking about the Tanach.[86]

Certain questions began forming in my mind. If the Tanach was the Word of God, why do so many churches hardly study it beyond occasional references? Why was it relegated to certain stories for children's Sunday school classes? Why were certain Hebrew words mistranslated into English? Who did this? Who compiled "The Bible"? Why were certain books selected and others left out? In fact, why were some letters from Paul used as the bulk of the New Testament? I attempted to learn more deeply from the writings of Paul but all it did was leave me confused.

Being immersed in the Tanach and attempting to navigate a New Testament church was a paradox. We attended Bible studies and Sunday sermons and found them to be very shallow. Our continued desire for a closer connection with God and deeper study into

---

[86] Hebrew Bible

actual Scripture (the Tanach) was still unmet. All we were given were canned sermons and people called us Bible nerds.

I distinctly recall a time when we were sitting in the church when the pastor announced another pre-packaged sermon series on tithing called "Plastic Donuts." My husband and I gave each other the look, "Seriously?" This increased our sense of disconnect. We stopped tithing to this church and then realized where we really stood. It was just like any other dues-paying club.

As we questioned the modern-day Christian church, Jewish themes and references were coming up in various prophecy conferences that we listened to in an attempt to learn from the prophetic writings. At this point, we were drawn into the Hebrew Roots/ Messianic movement. We were immersed in learning the Torah (from their perspective), the Hebrew language and the Jewish festivals. We learned about the pagan roots of the so-called Christian holidays. Our inner radar hadn't alerted us that something was off about the whole movement as we were busy absorbing new information.

At this point, I decided to make it a priority for me and my family to go to Israel. It was always in my heart to go to Israel. We did not personally know any Jewish people and had only limited exposure to certain Jewish customs, laws and prayers, which were filtered through a Christian lens. I wanted to connect with and learn directly from the Jewish people. I set an intention that we would go there and meet Jewish people, develop friendships, volunteer, learn, see historical sites and enjoy the land.

And just like that, it happened! The three summers we went to Israel were defining moments in our growth. Every aspect of my intention was fulfilled. We made wonderful friendships with Jews, volunteered our time at vineyards and saw many historical locations. We mingled in the culture, learned from real rabbis and fell in love with the raw beauty of the land. **There was such a vitality and connection to God in everything that observant Jews did in life! This was exactly what I was seeking!**

I remember listening to a Jewish shop owner and teacher, so full of passion and excitement for God, for Israel and for being Jewish. I thought, "This man has more of a relationship with God than I've ever seen from any Christian." It stuck with me.

We came home changed people who were passionate about sharing with those around us the realities of life in Israel, her people and her beauty. We hosted Israel information nights, where we conducted presentations woven with pictures and told our experiences. We also hosted Israeli wine-tasting events. We opened our home to several Jewish friends who were on speaking tours. We had a purpose in supporting the Jewish people. I began taking Hebrew language classes, both on how to read Biblical Hebrew and conversational Hebrew. I longed for the same loving connection that I saw the Jews had to God.

Back at home base, interacting with Christians shined a light on my dichotomy. One uncomfortable situation was with Christian friends at a Bible study. I was relaying the beauty of the shop owner and his obvious connection with God and my friend's husband said, "He can't have a relationship with God." I felt like someone punched me in the stomach! How can a person say this? All because someone didn't accept Jesus as their lord and savior? My experience told me otherwise. Our Bible studies together ended.

We were experiencing a huge paradigm shift and our time with the Messianic churches revealed a sense of disconnect from our experience in Israel. There were certain things in the church, such as Shabbat and prayers that were familiar and good, but then there were other things caused me to feel ill at ease.

Their independent omer[87] count was one such case. As I attempted to understand why most Messianics counted the omer differently from the Jews, I was met with various explanations that were complicated narratives justifying their personal interpretation of the Torah. This left a very bad taste in my mouth. I thought, "Here are the Jewish people who have studied the Torah and preserved it for thousands of years and these Messianics are essentially telling the Jews they are wrong."

I decided to count the omer with the Jews while the unsettled feelings brewed inside me.

There was another instance where the pastor of one of the churches inserted his own prayer into the Shabbat liturgy. In one section, he specifically said, "That their [Jews'] eyes would be opened and that they will soon accept Yeshua as messiah." I *refused* to say this prayer! I brought it up to him and, to his credit, he removed it from the collective liturgy, but he said this was still ultimately his prayer.

This was another step in my understanding of who and what Messianics really stood for. As friendly and pro-Israel as this group claims to be, there's the underlying message that the Jews must accept Jesus for the coming redemption to take place.

Interestingly, the iconic symbology bothered me as well. I disliked seeing a Christian cross flag displayed next to the Israeli flag. I knew that Jews did not believe that Jesus was the son of God, nor the messiah. It felt disconcerting to see these two symbols next to each other, as though they were complementary. The image of the cross bothered me as well. It was used as a torture device. Why is it proudly displayed at the front of all these churches? I get that they

---

[87] Every evening from the second night of Passover until the day before Shavuot, Jews count the 49 days that connect these two holidays.

think this is where their salvation occurred, but I found it disturbing nonetheless.

In saying the Shema[88] prayer, I had questions about "Hashem echad - Hashem is *One*". What does this mean in relation to the Trinity? I knew the doctrine of the Trinity, but the trite explanations and analogies to eggs being three-in-one did not satisfy me. How could the concept of the Trinity hold any merit in light of so many Scriptures I read?

What about in the Book of Numbers where God states that He is not a man, nor mortal? What about the prophetic writings in Isaiah that clearly say there is no other God? What about Deuteronomy 4:35 which says that Hashem is God and there is nothing besides Him? Ein od milvado.[89]

With more unanswered questions stirring up inside me, I desired authentic teaching from a Jewish perspective and not from Christians, who filtered everything through the lens of Paul and the gospel writers. I listened to Jewish teachers such as Rabbi Michael Skobac with Jews for Judaism, AnaRina Bat Zion Kreisman with Align with Zion, Tamir Kreisman with The Tent of Abraham, Rabbi Jeremy Gimpel, Rabbi Ari Abramowitz, Moshe Kempinski, Rabbi Alon Anava and Rabbi Tovia Singer. More recently, I've learned from Rabbi Avraham Sutton, Shifra Hendrie and Rabbi Rachamim Bitton of Lev Emunah Therapy. I also had a Jewish friend, Eliezer Braun, of whom I could ask questions.

As I absorbed the ancient wisdom from these wonderful friends and teachers, my soul resonated with their words. I felt a change in perspective, which led to changes in my external world.

---

[88] The central assertion of the Oneness of God in Jewish liturgy
[89] Transliteration of the last three Hebrew words from Deuteronomy 4:35 that mean, "There is none else besides Him."

I learned more Hebrew by listening to their teachings. My eyes were opened to the many mistranslations from Hebrew to English of specific words and writings in the prophets. I became more aware of the *Oneness* of God and what this means. I received answers to my previous questions about who compiled the Christian Bible. I learned about the different layers of learning in the Torah (PaRDeS)[90] and dove in with both feet! While I continued to study, the beauty of the Torah unfolded even more.

The nagging issue in the back of my mind was Jesus. I knew that if I continued down this path, I would have to deal with this guy. What did I really believe about him and why? If I tugged on this thread, the whole tapestry would unravel. What held me back was a feeling of guilt about betraying him, which had been implanted in me from my childhood.

I finally came to the realization that the Messianic/Hebrew Roots movement was nothing more than another brand of Christianity with cherry-picked Jewish customs sprinkled in. When I brought my questions about Jesus to the pastor of the Messianic church he told me, "We came out of one ditch when we left Christianity and we need to be careful not to fall into the other ditch with the Jews rejecting Jesus." I was stunned. I grew up being taught the Jews have got it wrong, but to hear someone explicitly say that the People of *The* Book are wrong and that they, the Messianics, have got the whole truth was too much for me. This is what caused me to walk away. Exit stage left.

So I was on my own, which felt exhilarating. My mother was on her own journey and sent me "The Real Messiah and Why He Is Not Jesus," a playlist from Jews for Judaism. I listened to the whole thing in a day. This flipped the switch for me.

---

[90] a Jewish method of Biblical exegesis based on four levels of interpretation

I don't think there was one particular piece of evidence that caused me to let go; it was all the evidence presented by the people who have studied and *lived* the Torah for thousands of years. From the people who have suffered and died for the Torah at the hands of Christians. From the people who *know*.

Just like that, I let go. It didn't come with a drum roll or applause, just a quiet knowing and release. Once I took off the Jesus glasses, it was as though I was seeing things clearly for the first time. It's as though I could feel God's light, as though He said to me, "Here I am and I've been here all along." I came to know my Creator, without something in between blocking my relationship. It was pure and beautiful. It was real. It was true.

Tamir Kreisman published a weekly teaching series on his YouTube channel, called "The Red Series" where he systematically addressed the many problems and inconsistencies around Christianity and Jesus. He addressed all the reasons why Jesus doesn't fulfill the requirements to be Messiah, much less a deity. I was astounded to realize that the Jesus narrative is no more than a Roman Catholic repackaging of various stories of pagan gods such as Horus, Dionysus and Mithra. This series of teachings helped affirm my decision to leave all this behind.

About this same time, my family and I moved to Montana, which made the break up with the Messianics easier. I felt a huge sense of relief, a spiritual move and a physical move at the same time.

Sounds great, but then reality set in. Now what? Where do I go to find a connection? Do I convert to Judaism now? How do I explain this to my husband and son? My son is open to God and very discerning, so I first brought it up with him; he was on the same page as me! He told me that he never liked being in the Messianics but because he hadn't studied the topic, he didn't voice his objections.

When I shared with my husband, he was initially surprised and confused. Since he had recently begun a new job, he did not have the time to devote to his own study. He asked for time to process and learn as he could. I am so grateful that they both had open hearts to receive what I was sharing. I've known families where this was not the case and it is heartbreaking.

The year that followed was one of the darkest and lowest that I've ever experienced. I felt unmoored and lost without a spiritual community. The closest Jewish synagogue was a 2.5-hour drive in any direction. While I knew I would never go back to Christianity, I was feeling lonely. A barrage of thoughts and questions weighed heavily upon me. Where was my place? I missed meeting with a community on a regular basis. Where do I belong now? How do I share my experience with people? With whom? Is the next step to convert to Judaism? I slumped into a very deep sadness. I felt confused and stuck.

What happened next was a lifeline to a drowning soul. My friend AnaRina Kreisman and her husband Tamir began a weekly Zoom group to connect people who were either on the path to conversion or taking their place as a Noahide, of which I knew very little. The motto of our group is, "In the tent of Abraham, all are welcome, but leave your idols at the door." Tamir and AnaRina had been fielding so many questions and hearing similar stories from people that they felt this was imperative. I am forever grateful to them for their time, their efforts, their love and their energy, which they have poured into helping bring home the sparks of holiness and helping lost and lonely Noahides.[91]

After conversations with AnaRina, I realized that my current situation did not allow for a path to conversion. This made me sink

---

[91] *Noahides* are non-Jews who follow the Seven Laws of Noah according to the Torah

even lower into apathy. In this valley, I cried out to God a lot. I cried like a child throwing a tantrum! I was so confused. What in the world am I doing? What's the point? I had a vague awareness of the Seven Noahide Laws, thanks to a Jewish man who gave me a brochure at the Cave of Machpelah[92]. In reading through the brochure, this path seemed like a cop-out to me, as though I was settling for being less than, for not achieving the highest and best I could be. It felt very unsatisfying to consider.

Another component that I had to address was the gross appropriation of Jewish laws and customs which I learned were not meant for non-Jews. There were certain prayers and blessings that I should not be saying. I don't have to keep kosher. Non-Jewish men shouldn't wear a kippah or tzitziot. After learning from a Chabad rabbi and reading in the book *The Divine Code*, I understood that I should not attempt to observe the Shabbat (not that I *ever* fully kept the Shabbat). And in fact, I shouldn't even attempt to celebrate Passover.

I felt like a fool. I was embarrassed and ashamed that I had come along and taken something that was not mine. I felt like a complete failure with things that I was sincerely trying to do to connect to God. These traditions were the few things that I felt I had left in connecting me to Judaism. But I swallowed my pride and let go. I did teshuva[93] for my arrogance and appropriation.

Nevertheless, I was now stranded as to how to practically live. Even though my family had agreed on our move and had been initially happy about our new home, I began to feel resentment towards this decision and my family too. Sadness became a cloak. This line of thought and unhappiness couldn't continue; my low mood was affecting everyone around me.

[92] The Cave of the Matriarchs and Patriarchs in Hevron (Hebron)
[93] repented

I continued crying out to God but not from a place of desperation, but more from a place of emunah.[94] God hears and answers all prayers and with this confidence, I was able to move forward another little step and attend a six-week class with a Chabad rabbi to discuss the Noahide laws.

My takeaway from this class was that Noahides do not attend Chabad nor synagogues, nor do we participate in any mitzvot given only to Israel. The rabbi shared how the Seven Laws can be unpacked and there is a lot more depth to them than just a quick read at face value. This was satisfying to hear. A difficult pill to swallow was when we were told that we needed to find our own leader. I was initially affronted, but then I felt a small release. God would guide me and continue to provide teaching and leadership. If he can use me in this, I wanted to be open and willing.

Throughout this journey, I have and always will see Israel and my Jewish friends like a big brother or sister. I'm not part of the Nation of Israel, but I know that they are who God chose to share the light of the Torah to the Nations. They are the people who accepted the Torah before even knowing what was in it! This has never wavered in my heart and mind. In the geula, the coming redemption, I see myself in the role of a Noahide, helping and supporting in any way possible. I don't have a clear vision of what this looks like, however, I know that if I keep on learning and doing what Hashem has for me to do, that my path will continue to unfold as it always has!

I maintain a close connection with several Jewish friends, some who have been with me on my journey from the beginning and others who have come alongside me and applauded me as a Noahide. Eliezer and Ellen Braun and Tamir and AnaRina Kreisman are friends I can reach out to for a quick hello or a deeper conversation.

---

[94] faith

I've been welcomed by Rabbi Bitton of Lev Emunah Therapy, who has helped me on my healing journey. The women in this community have accepted and embraced me as an equal and think I'm very special for being the only Noahide (for now) in this community!

Along this new path, there have been many different types of reactions from Christian friends and family. I have lost several friends. I've had some people attempt to proselytize me back to Christianity. I've been challenged with rapid-fire questioning as though I was on trial! Others with whom I've shared seem so perplexed that they just ignore my words. There are some friends who know where I stand and just avoid the topic altogether.

Recently, I made the step of taking the Noahide proclamation[95] with Rabbi Moshe Peres of the Noahide Academy of Israel. It brought me to a new level of inner peace and joy. I felt tremendously grateful and proud to publicly renounce idolatry in front of a beit din and take my place in this journey of mine. I honored my soul with this declaration. I would highly recommend that anyone who has accepted their path as a Noahide take the time to do this. It felt like a seal of approval from Hashem.

Today, I stand with my chin up and happily embrace being a Noahide. I'm excited to see how life unfolds and desire to be at the front of this change. If every human truly embraced the Seven Noahide Laws, this world would be transformed in an instant! My intention is to help facilitate this new reality shift.

If you are feeling confused in your walk and unsure if you are meant to convert or to accept the Noahide path, start by considering something that AnaRina and Tamir say, "Does your soul feel a part of *Am Yisrael*?" This is nuanced if you've come from the Messianics

---

[95] A statement made in front of a Jewish court of three by a non-Jew who agrees to uphold the seven universal Noahide Laws.

with their cultural appropriation. Someone can feel that they are meant to convert, but do not have the self-discipline, sacrifice, commitment or general life situation to do so. Be absolutely honest with yourself about this.

I admit that my ego was in the way of accepting myself as a Noahide. This was due to my insecurity in my relationship with God, a residual effect of my Christian upbringing. This was another point of releasing an old self-limiting belief which brought me into new peace and security of God's limitless love for me. When we accept where Hashem has positioned each one of us, then we can be the very best version of ourselves, finding purpose and wholeness.

The most recent phase of my journey was connecting with Rabbi Rachamim Bitton. He was a guest speaker at an online summit with Shifra Hendrie. What he shared at that summit was like a lightning bolt that hit me. By working with him, I've learned how to heal from my past, dissolve blocks that were hindering my growth and transform my life.

I was always perplexed by the concept of tikkun olam, rectifying the world. I never understood how we were meant to do this. Only now, understanding that I am a microcosm of the entire universe does this make sense. If each one of us learned how to heal and "sweeten the judgment" as Rabbi Bitton says, this world would transform in an instant! There is no other work that matters and is central to my feeling of purpose today.

My journey has felt slow, with periods of time feeling stuck; however, I was and continue to move forward. Overall, my path has gently unfolded as I persevered, learned, applied the learning, stepped forward and aligned my life with the learning. My feelings about my journey are expressed perfectly in the song "Unbroken" by the Jewish country singer, Joe Buchanan. He wrote, "You're unchained, you're unbroken, you're unbound. So lift your head up high and you can smile, and show God your face even if it's been a while. So raise your glass and stand tall 'cause you are made of love after all."

Today, my family and I do not have a physical spiritual community. The three of us know our role as Noahides so we live accordingly. We do not attend any religious gatherings in person anywhere, so there is still a feeling of being disconnected and unmoored. However, I have my communities online with our Tent of Abraham family and Lev Emunah family. I work as a facilitator and transformation coach with Lev Emunah and it is so exciting to help people in their personal healing journey.

In terms of the Noahide path, I am always willing to share as I discern someone with a spark and a desire to learn more. I've found what I was searching for, a deeper connection and relationship with my God. As with leaving behind all things Christian, this was a quiet and simple transition into accepting my place. I continue to embrace who I am, a proud Noahide.

Vanessa is a recovering public school educator. She grew up in Western Washington State and has made her current home in Big Sky Country, Montana, USA. She is a student of Rabbi Bitton in Jerusalem, Israel and a certified facilitator with his school, Lev Emunah Therapy. She inspires people to break free from apathy, reclaim their power, and transform their lives into something extraordinary.

If you would like to connect with Vanessa to chat or find out how she can help you in your transformation journey, you may reach her at vanessa@expansivelifesolutions.com.

How An Aversion to Halloween Led Me to Torah

Martina Zelenak

My name is Martina Zelenak. I am from Germany and moved to Texas in 1997. In Germany, I grew up knowing religion superficially. For many Germans, including myself, attending a church was something you did because everyone did it. Many Germans show up in church for weddings, funerals and little else. It was mostly ritual, with little or no personal connection to faith.

As for me, I had no relationship with Jesus growing up, but I knew that there was a Creator. In 1998, I started to attend a Baptist church. That is where I confessed my faith in Jesus. This was the first time I entered a "relationship" with "my god".

I believed in my Creator but also in Jesus. For the next 23 years, this was the path I followed. Wanting to get closer to Jesus, I sought to serve him and started a preschool at a Baptist church near Nashville, Tennessee, where I was a member. I served as the director of the preschool for 16 years. I enjoyed teaching the children their bible stories, and took that class on, in addition to my functions as the director at the school. The most enjoyable times were centered around celebrating the holidays, except for one, with the children,

I've always had an aversion to Halloween. It just seemed so dark to me and I had a difficult time understanding why adults enjoyed it as much as if not more than the children. During my time as director, I managed to keep the celebration of Halloween out of my preschool. However, over the course of my tenure as director, things changed in the church.

In 2019, the church planned to have a trunk or treat[96] event as an outreach to the community. I grudgingly agreed to set up a booth. My husband, Dan, and I went to YouTube to get some ideas for decorating our trunk. After looking at a couple of videos, we came to one in which a person was interviewing people attending a trunk or treat. As the video progressed the person pointed out the evil represented by the decorations. He asked the people at the booths what Jesus might think of the scene.

This had me wondering why I agreed to participate in the church's event. The next day, I saw a posting on my neighborhood's social media and that was the last straw. The post spoke of the evils of Halloween and included a link to a video that documented the pagan history of the holiday. This was my "second witness". I felt I was being led by the "Holy Spirit".

After watching the video, I questioned first why churches participate in Halloween as a way to reach people for Jesus and how could embracing the holidays "bring light to the darkness". Immediately, my husband and I withdrew from being hosts at the trunk or treat event. I went on further and managed to get the event changed into a "fall festival" on a night other than Halloween. This was just the first "shot across the bow".

Dan and I dug deeper and looked into the history of all the

---

[96] Halloween candy is handed out from the trunks of vehicles instead of door-to-door

"holidays" we celebrated. To my disbelief, I discovered the pagan origin of Easter as a fertility ritual and Christmas as the birthday of a Roman sun god. We couldn't believe the hypocrisy! The church had lost most of its credibility in our eyes, which lead us to stop going to church at that point.

Together, Dan and I started searching. We asked ourselves if there were festivals in the bible that we should be celebrating. Our journey into the Hebrew Roots had begun.

Armed with little more than the names you hear in public for "Jewish" festivals, such as Passover, Rosh Chodesh[97], Chanukah, etc., we asked Mr. Google where information about them appeared in the "Old Testament". This quickly led to Leviticus 23.

Excited, we wanted to celebrate the feasts we found there. Having no idea how to go about it, we researched and ultimately purchased a book on the Biblical Feasts. The book had been written by a person from the Hebrew Roots perspective. We had found a gold mine! I remember how special our first Passover was. COVID had shut down the world, so we made our own Haggadah[98] and followed the instructions in the Biblical Feast book. I know now that it was a mixture of Judaism and Christianity, the sacred and the profane. However, that Passover had so much more meaning than any Easter ever had to us.

COVID turned out to be a blessing for me. With physical services at church on hold for the foreseeable future, as well as the preschool being shutdown, I had time to think. More importantly, I had time to pray and read.

In August of 2020 I decided to leave my position as a director

---

[97] Rosh Chodesh marks the beginning of each Hebrew month

[98] The traditional text read at a Passover Seder, telling about the Israelites Exodus from Egypt

at the preschool and the church itself. I just couldn't bring myself to continue working at a place that had become the antithesis of faith for me. This decision brought both relief and sadness. I was freed from the lies and distortion, but I was also freed from a number of old friends. One incident in particular stood out among the early losses.

I had a close friend who had been a teacher at my preschool. We had been through so much over the years. We had been through divorces, we cried, we laughed, we prayed. We were family. It happened on one of our Friday dinner and game nights that Dan and I started talking about the changes in our beliefs. The conversation soon turned negative. They said we were on a very dangerous road and being terribly deceived. It got to the point that my dear friend said that she felt attacked and upset, and needed leave immediately.

I had learned the first lesson of HaShem's call. Not everyone would "correct" their beliefs, no matter how wrong I told them they were. This last year, we learned the same all over again. We finally realized that HaShem is One, He has no equal, and He need not require the death of an innocent, perfect "son" to redeem His people.

Dan and I planned a trip to Israel during the Sukkot Feast in 2023. We were in Israel on October 7th when that horrific attack on the Jewish people took place. It was our last day in Israel. We had spent three weeks in Israel and had connected to the Land of Israel and the people. We enjoyed our time there, but were still happy to be heading home.

On the morning of October 7th, Dan climbed to the top of a rock outcrop in the Arava[99], near the place where we were staying. He heard the sounds of explosions in the kibbutzim[100] near Gaza,

---

[99] An area in the Negev desert, south of the Dead Sea
[100] Israeli communities

but attributed the sounds to IDF training elsewhere in the Arava. Later that morning, we heard the initial reports of the attack, little was known of what had happened.

The place we were staying in the Arava was Biblical Tamar Park, a national park in the Israeli National Park system. It was an oasis that had been host to many peoples since the Abrahamic period, the last being the British Army. Based on the little our tour guides had heard, they had us pack up early and head to Ben Gurion Airport. On the way there we received texts from our air carrier that they had suspended service to Israel and that our flights were canceled, (thanks a lot, Delta).

After a night near the airport, which included a brief stay in the stairwell/bomb shelter, we finally left Israel one day later. (Thank you so much El Al, the only airline I will ever fly on again, given a choice). We were detoured to England and finally, back to the United States.

When we heard the details of the attack, we were shocked. We couldn't believe how brutal this attack had been. I was so sad for the Jewish people and the whole situation. I just couldn't believe what had happened. I wished we were still in the land and were able to help somehow. I felt helpless being here in the US, unable to do anything.

We had gone to Israel with another couple with whom we had become close friends during our time in the Hebrew Roots movement. We had been through a lot with this couple, including separation from the Hebrew Roots congregation we had been in since 2020. Both of us realized that we were still going to "church", and that only the day had changed. Oh, we told ourselves we were following Torah, but we still believed in the deity of Jesus. Dan and I both had stopped automatically ending our prayers in his name though. As time proceeded, we saw changes in ourselves or our congregation or mostly both. We felt that our congregation had become too "churchy" and so we left.

Later that year, I met a wonderful elderly Jewish lady who eventually agreed to teach Dan and me Hebrew. That was not the only thing we learned. She brought so many points out as to the authenticity of Jesus and the "New Testament". After she raised the questions in our minds, I started researching on the internet "Why don't Jews believe in Jesus?"

I stumbled on the teachings of Rabbi Tovia Singer through the "TeNaK Talk" YouTube channel. Everything he said made so much sense. I eventually picked up his books, *Let's Get Biblical, Volumes 1 and 2*. This blew away what was left of Christianity in our hearts and minds.

We had discovered the most basic and profound piece of knowledge, which is that HaShem is One. He needs no other and no other was part of bringing His creation into being.

All this weighed heavily on me. I couldn't keep it to myself any longer. I finally confessed to my friend that Dan and I had to let go of Jesus and the New Testament. My friend and I were having lunch together and over the course of our conversation I told her how we questioned the New Testament and Jesus' divinity. A couple of days later, I received a text from her in which she said that her heart was broken for us. She said that the path that my husband and I were on was the path of deception. Further, she explained that the connecting link between us that we once had was gone. I had lost another "Best Friend". This was devastating to me.

I felt completely lost, a person without a country, family or friends. I still believed Dan and I were on the right path. HaShem had drawn us to Himself. The insight that we had into the Tanach[101],

---

[101] Hebrew scriptures

looking at through Jewish eyes instead of those of Paul, Matthew, John, etc. made us realize how much we had missed in all those years of Christianity. We realized that we could not go backward.

But the path forward was still hazy, at best.

It was in the winter of 2023 that I reconnected with a friend from our Hebrew Roots congregation. To my surprise and delight, I found out that Deborah had left that path as well. Further, she had found a group, The Mishnah Walk, run by Victor Schultz, that was on the same path that I thought we needed be on to proceed. I was ready immediately to jump in, but Dan dug his feet a little. I am not sure what was holding him back, but I took my time. He can dig his feet in if he feels like he's being pushed. Eventually, Dan came around and agreed to join The Mishnah Walk.

They have a wonderful rabbi, Yosef Eliyah, conducting their sessions on Rambam's Mishnah Torah, which we believe is a necessity. We had already been down the path of the blind following the blind in Hebrew Roots. We investigated some other options for our path forward, including being a Noahide. This path seemed lonely to us. Noahides don't seem to have congregations. We want more. We want to be part of a community. We want to belong.

Some months later, Deborah told us she had found a rabbi who was going to conduct classes online for those who were thinking about possibly converting. We are currently attending that class. However, we plan to wait until the conclusion of the class to make a decision on conversion. We have also started attending a synagogue as visitors. This has opened our eyes further. We need to make sure before entering the water, both figuratively and literally.

We have been asked why we are thinking about converting. That answer is still a little jumbled in our heads. But this much we know: we love HaShem with our whole heart, with all our soul, and all our might. We believe He will show us the best way to do that.

Martina Zelenak was born in Germany, moved to Texas in 1997 and to Tennessee in 2002. She has two adult sons. She worked as a preschool director for 17 years before she left the Baptist church. After journeying through Christianity and Hebrew Roots, Martina and her husband Dan are on a path to convert to Judaism. She can be reached at gmlinthicum@ gmail.com.

APPENDIX A

The Abrahamic Movement: The Ancient Jewish Faith Path You Didn't Know You're Already Almost On

Rabbi Yishai Fleisher

A New Vision for Biblical Faith

> *"This is what the LORD of Heaven's Armies says: In those days ten men from different nations and languages of the world will clutch at the corner of the garment of one Jew. And they will say, 'Please let us walk with you, for we have heard that God is with you."* Zechariah 8:23

T oday, so many people feel dissatisfied with their birth-given religious system because of questions of authenticity, elements of idolatry, overt anti-Israelism, antisemitism, and replacement theology. Moreover, people sense the powerful worldwide struggle for morality and truth and want to link together in a way that will help turn the tide. Millions seek a path that honors their spiritual aspirations, feels authentic and timeless, and respects the unique covenant they learned about in their scriptures - the bond between God and the Jewish people.

This essay proposes that a new, but actually very old, framework is being formed: **the Abrahamic Movement, a Torah-guided path for gentiles** that honors their distinct identity as God-following non-Jews and which shines a light on a path for millions of believers who yearn for a connection to Biblical wisdom and the God of Israel.

The Current Challenge

Right now, millions around the world are trying to find their way to true service of God. Many are following the Bible through their own interpretation but with no guidance. At the same time, many individual rabbis and thinkers are working to refine the Torah way for gentiles - and yet their work has not gelled into a cohesive movement.

Not yet.

With regards to the church, articles appear regularly talking about why millions of Christians are unsatisfied with their current faith path: "About 40 million Americans have left churches and other religious institutions in the last 25 years."

But why is this happening? There are various social reasons, but a percentage of that dissatisfaction comes from a loss of faith in the authenticity of Christian texts and practices. In some sects, there has been an effort to de-idolatrize Christian practices by removing things like Christmas. Others try to buttress Christianity by incorporating Orthodox Jewish practices into Christianity, such as wearing tzitzit, celebrating the Biblical feasts, and searching for the "Hebrew Roots" of the "New Testament." Yet others see the miraculous rebirth of Israel, see God's hand in it, and want to have a role in it.

This has brought about various forms of pro-Israelism in churches including Christians United for Israel (CUFI) and others. But for some, this is not enough. They sense the Church's stubborn antisemitism and replacement theology and they yearn for an authentic path to connect with Israel and with "what God is doing."

The Muslim world is much harsher in its response to change and challenges. However, it is precisely because of its political repression that people are looking for a new path: "A large survey conducted by the University of Michigan from 1981 to 2020 found that in countries like Tunisia, Morocco, and Iraq, many people who were traditionally Muslim now identify as atheists. In Lebanon, about 43% admitted they do not practice Islam in their private lives, although they may not express this openly due to the severe punishments for apostasy in Muslim-majority countries." Yet, even in Muslim countries like Iran, there is respect and love of Israel and a yearning for a new faith path that is authentic and that replaces Islamic oppression with a God of love and freedom - the God of Abraham.

Judaism's Initial Offering

Judaism's historical faith system offering to non-Jews is called the Noahide laws. Followers of these laws are called *Bnei Noach* meaning Children of Noah. This system is based on seven foundational commandments that were given to Noah and provide crucial ethical foundations for humanity. The seven laws of Noah are:

1. Prohibition of idolatry
2. Prohibition of blasphemy
3. Prohibition of murder
4. Prohibition of sexual immorality

5. Prohibition of theft
6. Prohibition of eating flesh from a living animal,
7. Requiring the establishment of courts of justice.

The Biblical roots of the Noahide laws are found in the covenant that God established with Noah after the Flood (see Genesis 9:1–17). The Torah does not list distinct commands, but the Sages used the statements of moral imperative found in these verses as a foundation for articulating the Noahide code. The first clear formulation of the Seven Noahide Laws is found in the Talmud's Tractate Sanhedrin 56a-60a.

The great 12ᵗʰ-century scholar and philosopher Maimonides (also known by the Hebrew acronym Rambam) was the first to codify a systematic legal presentation of the Noahide laws. In the section on "Laws of Kings and Wars" of his great legal work *Mishne Torah*, the Rambam devotes the better part of three chapters to the Seven Noahide Laws.

Not only does he give guidance on how to live by these laws, but he also emphasizes their spiritual importance saying that "anyone who accepts upon himself the fulfillment of these seven mitzvot and is precise in their observance is considered one of 'the pious among the gentiles' and will merit a share in the world to come…when he accepts them and fulfills them because the Holy One, blessed be He, commanded them in the Torah…" (Kings and Wars 8:11).

Over the past two centuries, the concept of non-Jews embracing the Noahide laws has evolved from a theoretical Biblical structure into an organized movement. The turning point in that process is thought to be the publication of the 1914 *Israel and Humanity* by Italian rabbi and kabbalist Elijah Benamozegh (1822-1900). His work advocates the adoption of a universal moral code based on the Seven Noahide Laws, offering believers a bridge between Judaism and the broader world. Using a Kabbalistic cosmology, his system promoted Noahide religious universalism alongside a dedicated Orthodox Judaism.

In the latter half of the 20th century, the idea gained momentum through the efforts of Rabbi Menachem Mendel Schneerson, the seventh Lubavitcher Rebbe. His encouragement among non-Jews of the Noahide laws as a foundation for ethical living became the "7 for 70" campaign – 7 laws for the 70 nations. The campaign reached its height when, in 1991, the US Congress passed a joint resolution recognizing the Noahide laws as "the bedrock of society from the dawn of civilization" and honoring the Rebbe's efforts to promote them as a source of ethical values.

Since then, other voices have arisen in favor of the promotion of a Noahide movement specifically and sharing Torah with the nations in general. These include the works of Rabbi Yitzchak Ginsburgh, Rabbi Eliezer Melamed, Rabbi Chaim Richman, Rabbi Shmuel Eliyahu, Rabbi Oury Cherki and more.

The Problem with Noahidism

However, the Noahide system proved insufficient as an alternative to current religious structures and never caught on big. As a system, it was too skeletal: it created no community, no regular worship, no shared celebrations, and no structured approach to divine service. We humans yearn for a faith path that helps us translate deep values into daily actions and we crave communal structures within which to share those values.

We want a religious system with integrity that is satisfying to us (and hopefully to the Lord), and yet with enough openness and flexibility to be adaptable. Noahidism did not provide these.

Moreover, the very term "Noahide" was a significant marketing obstacle in reaching spiritual seekers. While the Biblical Noah was righteous in his generation, he is not a compelling or relatable figure around whom to build a religious identity. Also, the term itself Noahide (the word "hide,"- is that running away? The skin of an animal?) is phonetically unattractive and fails to inspire a satisfying self-identification.

Lastly, Judaism did not evangelize the Noahide concept. The Jewish people have been in exile for the last 2,000 years and were not in the mindset to teach non-Jews how to serve God - nor were the gentiles listening. But with the Divine process of the ingathering of the exiles afoot, things are changing. Non-Jews are asking Jews for a path, and Jewish leaders with a heart for the nations know that the time for Israel's light to shine forth to the world has arrived.

Nothing More Organic Than Being Abrahamic

For the nations to receive Torah, it needs to be attractive. The term "Noahide," while being a legal category, could never have mass market appeal. In contrast to Noah and Noahide, the name **Abraham** and **Abrahamic** is much more attractive to Christians and Muslims alike. Abraham is universally recognized as the father of monotheism and his story provides an inspiring template for spiritual seekers.

For Jews, he is Avraham Avinu (Abraham our Father), the founder of the nation. For Muslims, he is Ibrahim Al-Khalil (Abraham the Friend of God), the great patriarch. For Christians, he is the father of faith whose trust in God became the model for all believers. Abraham's journey - leaving his father's house, discovering the one God, teaching truth to others, showing hospitality to strangers, and becoming a blessing to all nations - resonates deeply across cultures and traditions.

The great Rabbi Lord Jonathan Sacks writes: "Abraham is without doubt the most influential person who ever lived. Today he is claimed as the spiritual ancestor of 2.3 billion Christians, 1.8 billion Muslims and 14 million Jews, more than half the people alive today. Yet he ruled no empire, commanded no great army, performed no miracles and proclaimed no prophecy. He is the supreme example in all of history of influence without power. Why? Because he was prepared to be different. As the Sages say, he was called ha-ivri, "the Hebrew," because "all the world was on one side (be-ever echad) and he was on the other."

Standing before Israel's Knesset in January 2018, Vice President Mike Pence echoed Rabbi Sack's sentiments: "Nearly 4,000 years ago, a man left his home in Ur of the Chaldeans to travel here, to Israel. He ruled no empire, he wore no crown, he commanded no armies, he performed no miracles, delivered no prophecies, yet to him was promised 'descendants as numerous as the stars in the sky.' Today, Jews, Christians, and Muslims - more than half the population of the Earth, and nearly all the people of the Middle East - claim Abraham as their forefather in faith."

While religious communities may differ in many ways, the character of Abraham represents a shared foundation of faith that resonates across cultural and theological divides. In an era of spiritual seeking and global connection, perhaps it's time to build upon the common ground of Abraham in a new way.

The recent success of the "Abraham Accords" proves the enduring power of Abraham's name to bridge cultures and build a sense of commonality.

Let's put it all together: we propose that a new movement, based on the Torah's Noahide Laws but expanded to create a full religious life based for non-Jews be established. We believe that this "new religion" should be called the "Abrahamic Faith" or "House of Abraham," "Children of Abraham," or more simply: ABRAHAMIC.

To be clear: this system, as does Orthodox Torah-based Judaism, rejects the so-called New Testament and the Christian god. For that matter, this system rejects the Divine validity of the Quran as well. In places like the United States, which is a predominantly Christian country, there will be curiosity on the one hand as well as hostility on the other. The reason for hostility is obvious. But America is also in a deep search of the "Hebrew roots" of the dominant faith - and potentially there will be millions who choose an authentic Torah-based (non-Christian) path, community, and life.

Building on Existing Foundations

Now, one may think that a new religion called the 'Abrahamic movement' is a radical innovation - but it is actually one of Judaism's oldest ideas. Avraham went to the Promised Land to teach about One God at the crossroads of the ancient world, and there he received the Divine covenant which made him "father of many nations." In the land of Israel, Abraham founded a particular people, known today as the Jewish people, to lead this vision, but their mission of teaching the path of Abraham remained universal. The Abrahamic vision of all peoples serving One God is an inheritance that humanity was always destined to receive.

There has been a lot of work done to bring together the knowledge and the framework for the Abrahamic Movement. Rivkah Lambert Adler, a pioneer educator and author in this field, has compiled an extensive bibliography of works dedicated to Torah teaching for gentiles. These include Rabbi Oury Cherki's *Brit Olam: Prayer*

Book for Noahides (2015), Rabbi Avraham Greenbaum's *Universal Torah: Lessons for Humanity from the Weekly Torah Readings* (2018), Rabbi David Katz's *Laws of Ger Toshav: Pious of the Nations* (2017), and Rabbi Yitzchak Ginsburgh's *Kabbalah and Meditation for the Nations*.

Hopefully, the Abrahamic movement will manage to unify these established resources - including existing books of religious law (halacha), prayer services, and educational frameworks. These will create clear pathways for Gentiles seeking to connect with Torah wisdom and practice.

A Living Calendar, A Living Faith

At the heart of this renewed Abrahamic movement lies the Jewish calendar - not merely as a way of marking time, but as a sophisticated spiritual system that transforms daily life. As Rav Mike Feuer, renowned Jerusalem educator and scholar of Jewish history, teaches: the Hebrew calendar blends the cyclical nature of festivals with the forward march of history, creating what he calls "a spiral of spiritual growth."

Through this calendar, Abrahamic believers will participate in the Biblical *moadim* - "appointed times for divine encounters" - and join Israel and Jews around the world in celebration. Indeed, each festival, fast day, and Sabbath carries profound significance, and sharing those times with family, friends and believers around the world will create a strong community bound to the authentic, age-old tradition.

For example: Passover commemorates not only the exodus of the Jewish people but the universal idea of freedom and liberation from all forms of slavery. Shavuot (Pentecost / Weeks) marks the giving of the Torah's universal wisdom. Sukkot, traditionally a time for all nations to gather in Jerusalem, celebrates Divine protection and joy.

But when are these holidays exactly? Are average people supposed to guess when Passover takes place? By sharing a calendar based on Jewish wisdom, Abrahamics will be able to celebrate in the proper time.

But how exactly are these holidays to be celebrated by gentiles? There must be a unified set of laws and customs developed by Jewish and non-Jewish scholars working together to address how Abrahamics are supposed to celebrate these feasts and other rituals.

Halacha: Addressing Life's Deepest Questions

The renewed Abrahamic movement must provide comprehensive religious guidance through the development of specific halachic (Jewish legal) guidelines for the nations. This body of law should address the fundamental questions that the Noahide system left unanswered: How should Gentiles observe the Sabbath? What are the parameters of family purity laws? Should Gentile followers place mezuzahs on their doorposts? Should they practice circumcision?

These aren't merely practical questions - they represent deep engagement with Divine wisdom. While some basic principles are clear (such as Gentiles not being obligated to the full letter of Sabbath observance), many nuanced questions require careful consideration. This intellectual engagement will provide followers with both practical guidance and spiritual enrichment, making the Abrahamic path intellectually satisfying as well as spiritually fulfilling.

The development of Abrahamic halacha is key to the movement's commitment to providing a complete religious framework. Rather than leaving followers to interpret Biblical laws on their own, Abrahamic Law will give clear guidance to followers while maintaining appropriate distinctions between Jewish and Gentile obligations and identities.

Another major issue is the rejection of Christianity (and Islam for that matter). Abrahamics must be ready to explain why the movement does not accept the so-called "New Testament." Indeed, there will be many people who will try to be Abrahamic yet still hold on to the Christian faith and texts. However, while the movement must have an open door for discussion with people in search of truth, it must also hold strong against the strong tide of Christianity.

The Abrahamic Movement has arrived to challenge establishment religions with an authentic Jerusalem and Torah-based path for the nations which rejects idolatry and replacement theology.

The Stuff of a Renewed Movement

What will this new movement look like? The Abrahamic movement will provide a comprehensive religious system and communal structure for non-Jews, guided by Jewish teaching and with a face towards Jerusalem. The rabbis and Bible-loving non-Jews who are leading the Abrahamic consciousness are already creating regular communal prayer services, particularly on the Sabbath.

The Abrahamic Movement should establish a "franchise" of Houses of Abraham in communities worldwide, particularly in North America, where openness to spiritual innovation and a yearning for authentic "Hebrew roots of Christianity" create fertile ground. Each house will serve as a center for prayer, study, and community, led by qualified instructors providing authentic and accredited teaching. These houses of worship will be homes where believers can congregate and have fellowship, marry each other, and raise children as proud Abrahamics.

Annual Abrahamic pilgrimages to Jerusalem, especially on the Sukkot holiday, as prophesied in the book of Zecharia, will be the highlight of the year - creating an aliyah, a going up, of body and soul to Jerusalem and then bringing that Godly light back to all four corners of the world.

Leadership and teaching will come through complementary channels: local Jewish and non-Jewish instructors who have mastered the Abrahamic Faith and have a heart for all believers, online learning from Israel-based teachers, and an international clergy from all backgrounds trained in teaching and developing the practical application of the Torah to all people.

The Abrahamic movement will establish a certification program for lay leaders, providing thorough training in Jewish texts, traditions, and teachings appropriate for gentile communities. This approach aims to ensure an authentic transmission of Torah wisdom that is accessible to anyone and clarifies the details of daily service, customs, and obligations.

These Abrahamic communities will be linked through modern technology to a central headquarters in Jerusalem, where Israeli rabbis and lay leaders will provide guidance and teaching. Through internet broadcasts, live streams, and social media, the prophetic vision of Torah flowing forth from Zion will find new fulfillment. Followers will maintain constant connection with Jerusalem through daily news updates, virtual Torah classes, and regular visual links to the Holy City. The Abrahamic movement will utilize to the fullest the Godly gift of technology which enable a direct, immediate connection between Jerusalem and the furthest corners of the earth, as Isaiah 11:9 teaches:

"For the earth shall be full of the knowledge of the LORD, as the waters cover the sea."

A Vision of Global Transformation

Rabbi Oury Cherki writes: "Throughout history, the Jewish nation has been a spiritual catalyst, promoting universal values through its national and religious lifestyle. This destiny, which began with the message to Avraham that 'all the families of the earth shall be blessed through you,' is coming to life today, manifested in the return to Zion and the State of Israel."

Indeed, now, as Jerusalem is being rebuilt and Israel flourishes, Torah for the nations is coming forth as prophesied in Isaiah 2:3: "For out of Zion shall go forth the law, and the word of the LORD from Jerusalem."

God, in His infinite mercy, has granted us a spiritual path for gentiles seeking to serve the God of Israel. As Jerusalem's prominence and centrality grows and God's revelation becomes increasingly apparent, this movement stands ready to unite believers around a Biblical faith path that creates community, belonging, and purpose for gentiles and connects them to the heart of Israel.

This is the revitalization and realization of Abraham's original mission: teaching Divine truth to all peoples in a way that honors their unique role in God's great plan. With modern technology enabling unprecedented connections between gentiles around the world and Jerusalem, the Abrahamic movement has the potential to impact millions - and the light of Torah will truly illuminate the world from Zion.

Surely, the time has come for Israel to embrace its role as a light unto the nations, offering spiritual guidance to a world in desperate need of direction. The choice before us is clear: continue with insufficient frameworks that leave spiritual hunger unsatisfied or embrace this opportunity to create communities of faith centered on Jerusalem and biblical truth. God's gift of connecting technology is ready.

Will We Answer the Call?

The steps forward and the call to action are clear: to establish a central website and YouTube channel, to gather teachers and books in one central teaching hub, to open the first Abrahamic House in the US. These are the initial steps in a global revolution. If you want to be part of it, contact me at Yishai@yishaifleisher.com and prepare yourself to receive the gift of helping unlock God's vision for the nations of the world.

Rabbi Yishai Fleisher is the International Spokesperson for the Jewish Community of Hebron - a Middle East hotspot, King David's first capital, and home of the Mearat Hamachpela - the Tomb of the Biblical Patriarchs and Matriarchs. He is also an elected Councilman in one of the largest Jewish communities in Judea - Efrat. Rabbi Yishai is a popular English-language podcaster and YouTuber on the topics of Israel, Judaism, and the Middle East and has appeared in major media outlets including CNN, Piers Morgan, and more. Yishai is a rabbi, a graduate of Cardozo Law School in NYC, a former paratrooper, and continues to serve in the IDF reserves.

APPENDIX B

A Jewish Mystical View of Jesus[102]

———————— *Rivkah Lambert Adler, Ph.D.*

The world is destined to exist for six thousand years: two thousand years of tohu, two thousand years of Torah, and two thousand years of the days of the Messiah.- Talmud Sanhedrin 97a

There is a Talmudic teaching that this world will exist for 6000 years. The 6000 years are divided into three periods of 2000 years each. The first 2000 years, before the giving of the Torah, are called tohu, which means chaos or nothingness. The second 2000 years are called Torah because during that period, Avraham taught the world about monotheism, the Torah was given on Mount Sinai, the Tabernacle was constructed and inaugurated and the first two Holy Temples were built in Jerusalem.

---

[102] This essay is based on "The 2,000-year-old Klipah of Moshiach" by Devorah Fastag.

The Messianic Era

The last 2000-year period is called the period of Moshiach[103]. But if the Jews are still waiting for the Messiah, which we believe is the Messiah for the whole world, how is this an accurate name for this time period?

According to Rashi, the Messiah did not come at the end of the fourth millennium because of our sins. The final two millennia, which were supposed to have been the Messianic era, have turned out differently; the true Messiah has still not come.

The beginning of the Messianic era should have been the era of Moshiach ben Yosef (Messiah son of Joseph). Moshiach ben Yosef is the preparatory messianic figure who operates very much within the laws of nature.

To illustrate this idea, consider the growth in Israel's Jewish population. In May 1948, when the State of Israel was declared, approximately 650,000 Jews lived in the Land of Israel. In May 2025, approximately 7.7 million Jews were living in Israel. This is clearly a partial fulfillment of the prophecy of the ingathering of the exiles.

While this population explosion can be seen as a dramatic achievement, it occurred in the natural world. People crossed deserts or boarded boats and airplanes from other countries and landed in Israel to begin their lives. This is the work of Moshiach ben Yosef. So although we haven't identified a specific person as Moshiach ben Yosef, messianic advancements are proceeding in the natural world under the power of Moshiach ben Yosef.

By contrast, the period that will be led by Moshiach ben David[104] will be miraculous, beginning with the revival of the dead and con-

---

[103] Messiah

[104] Messiah son of David

tinuing with restoring the world to the elevated spiritual status it had in the Garden of Eden, before the sin of the eating of the Tree of Knowledge.

Two thousand years ago, the potential for revealing the true Messiah was not fulfilled because the world was not ready. Instead, the world got a false messianic figure.

In Jewish mystical thought, when a great spiritual opportunity is missed, its energy doesn't simply vanish—negative forces can take it over. Instead of entering a redemptive phase, this unfulfilled potential was misdirected and became a counterfeit version of the messianic era.

The counterfeit was the rise of a new religion centered around a Jew named Yeshua (Jesus). From a traditional Jewish point of view, this individual, though born into a Jewish context and initially trained in Torah, deviated from the path of Torah.

Christianity claims that he is the messiah. Most Christians believe that many foundational Torah laws are no longer necessary or relevant. The vast majority of Christians believe that the Jewish people lost their special relationship with God and that, as followers of Jesus/Yeshua, they are now the "true Israel" or the "spiritual Israel" or the "new Israel," replacing the Jews as God's chosen nation.

While these teachings had catastrophic consequences for the Jewish people who experienced centuries of persecution in the name of Christianity, some Jewish thinkers, including the renowned medieval Torah scholar and philosopher Maimonides[105], acknowledged that Christianity moved many people away from paganism and introduced them to concepts rooted in Torah, such as monotheism, moral law and the idea that a messianic personality will eventually redeem the world.

---

[105] Commonly known as the Rambam. Died in 1204.

Aisav and Yeshua

In Kabbalah[106], Jesus/Yeshua is considered a reincarnation of Aisav[107], a biblical figure who appeared outwardly righteous but was deeply flawed. Like Aisav, Yeshua is seen as someone with access to spiritual greatness who misused it. This connection is deepened when considering that the Hebrew spelling of Yeshua is a permutation of the Hebrew spelling of Aisav (עשיו – ישוע).

Jesus Appeared To Me

How does Torah thinking answer the claim of people who report having had direct encounters with Jesus/Yeshua?

There is a mystical Torah principle called klipah, meaning shell. In Kabbalah, for every force of holiness, there exists a counterpart on the side of impurity. Just as there are true prophets and genuine spiritual visions, there are also false ones. Similarly, there are spiritual experiences that come from impure sources. Even when people experience strong feelings or visions, Jewish tradition cautions that not all spiritual experiences come from a holy place.

Yehoshua and Yeshua: A Case of Mistaken Legacy

One of the central figures in the Hebrew Bible is Yehoshua[108], the student and successor of Moshe[109]. He led the Israelites into the

---

[106] Jewish mystical teaching

[107] Esau

[108] Joshua

[109] Moses

land of Israel, fought their enemies, and helped establish the Torah as the foundation of national life.

Yehoshua is viewed in Jewish tradition as an early expression of the soul of Moshiach ben Yosef. He fulfilled several tasks associated with Moshiach ben Yosef. One was to ensure that the Nation of Israel studied Torah and remained loyal to it. As Moshe's chief student, Yehoshua helped ensure the survival of the Torah.

Moshiach ben Yosef is also meant to fight the enemies of the Nation of Israel and Yehoshua did this as well. Moshiach ben Yosef is also charged with returning the Nation of Israel to the Land of Israel and, of course, Yehoshua did that too.

However, according to ancient teachings, Yehoshua failed to pray for the removal of the inclination toward idol worship. Centuries later, Jewish leaders known as the Men of the Great Assembly did pray for this, and their prayer was answered. The desire for idol worship was removed from the world, but the end of prophecy came with it. In Jewish theology, this is part of a balance: eliminating one spiritual force often requires giving up its opposite as well.

Because Yehoshua did not pray for the end of idol worship when he had the chance, the Bible refers to him by the shortened name Yeshua.

> *And all the congregation of the returnees from the captivity made booths and dwelt in the booths, for they had not done so from the days of* **Yeshua the son of Nun** *until that day, and there was exceedingly great joy.* – Nechemiah 8:17

This foreshadows the rise of a different Yeshua, who would come to be worshipped by two billion people worldwide. Some see this as a hint that, if Yehoshua had prayed for an end to idol worship, a different Yeshua would never have appeared.

A Hopeful Conclusion

The Jewish view expressed in these teachings sees history as full of spiritual potential and peril. Moments of missed spiritual opportunity can lead to false messiahs, misdirected energy and great suffering. Yet the belief remains strong that the true Messiah will eventually come, not one who abolishes the Torah or replaces Israel, but one who fulfills ancient prophecies and brings peace and truth to all humanity.

This vision is not one of vengeance or rejection, but of healing and clarity. The hope is for a time when confusion will end, spiritual truths will no longer be hidden behind klipot (shells), and all people will come to recognize the One Creator and Sustainer of the universe and walk in His ways.

Bibliography

Adler, Rivkah Lambert. *Ten From The Nations: Torah Awakening Among Non-Jews*. Geula Watch Press, 2017 and 2022.

Adler, Rivkah Lambert. *Lighting Up The Nations: Jewish Responsibility Towards the Nations Today and in the Messianic Era*. Geula Watch Press, 2021.

Bar-Ron, Rabbi Michael Shelomo. *Guide for the Noahide: A Complete Guide to the Laws of the Noahide Covenant and Key Torah Values for All*. Lightcatcher Books, 2010.

Bindman, Rabbi Yirmeyahu. *The Seven Colors of the Rainbow: Torah Ethics for Non-Jews*. Resource Publications, Inc., 2024.

Cherki, Rabbi Oury. Brit Olam: *Prayer Book for Noahides*. Noahide World Center, 2015.

Clorfene, Chaim and David Katz. *The World of the Ger*. 2004.

Clorfene, Chaim and Yakov Rogalsky. *The Path of the Righteous Gentile*. 2016.

Cowen, Shimon Dovid. *The Theory & Practice of Universal Ethics: The Noahide Laws*. The Institute for Judaism and Civilization, 2015.

Dallen, Michael Ellias. *The Rainbow Covenant: Torah and the Seven Universal Laws.* Lightcatcher Books, 2003.

Federow, Rabbi Stuart. *Judaism and Christianity: A Contrast.* 2012.

Federow, Rabbi Stuart. *The Real Reasons Why Jews Don't Believe in Jesus.* 2024.

Feld, Rabbi Avraham and OvadYah Avrahami. *Jewish Secrets Hidden in the New Testament: The growing global Torah revolution.* Eldad Publishers, Jerusalem. 2013.

Katz, David. *Laws of Ger Toshav: Pious of the Nations.* 2017.

Klinghoffer, David. *Why The Jews Rejected Jesus.* Three Leaves Press, 2006.

Nuszen, Shannon. *I Once Was Lost: One Woman's Exodus From the Depths of the Church.* Beyneynu, 2025.

Norman, Asher. *Twenty-Six Reasons Why Jews Don't Believe in Jesus.* Black White and Read Publishing, 2008.

Reese, Rachel. *Who Is Our Yeshua? A Jewish Look at Christianity and the Messianic Movement.* 2022.

Singer, Tovia. *Let's Get Biblical!: Why doesn't Judaism Accept the Christian Messiah?* Outreach Judaism, 2021.

Taylor, Penina. *Scripture Twisting: A Course in Jewish-Christian Polemics.* 2013.

Weiner, Rabbi Moshe. *The Divine Code: The Guide to Observing the Noahide Code, Revealed from Mount Sinai in the Torah of Moses.* Ask Noah International, 2020.

Wood, Jr., James *Leaving Jesus: A Book Every Christian Should Have Read Before They Believed in Jesus,* 2012.

Thanks for reading *Adrift Among The Nations: Between Christianity and Torah.* Please consider leaving an honest review on Amazon.com to help guide prospective readers.